LORD JONATHAN SUMPTION is a British judge and historian. He served as a Justice of the Supreme Court until 2018 and is the author of the *Sunday Times* bestseller *Trials of the State* and *Divided Houses*, which won the 2009 Wolfson History Prize.

ALSO BY JONATHAN SUMPTION

Trials of the State

Divided Houses

LAW IN A TIME OF CRISIS

JONATHAN SUMPTION

P

PROFILE BOOKS

This paperback edition published in 2022

First published in Great Britain in 2021 by
Profile Books Ltd
29 Cloth Fair
London
ECIA 7JQ
www.profilebooks.com

10 9 8 7 6 5 4 3 2 1

Typeset in Dante by MacGuru Ltd
Printed and bound in Great Britain by
CPI Group (UK) Ltd, Croydon, CR0 4YY

A CIP catalogue record for this book is available from the British Library.

ISBN 978 1 78816 712 3
eISBN 978 1 78283 807 4

CONTENTS

FOREWORD

These essays are based on lectures which I have given over the past decade, before, during and since my time as a Justice of the Supreme Court. They are all loosely concerned with law and public affairs in the broadest sense of those terms. I have updated them so that they speak as of 2020. In a few cases I have also added observations which I would not have felt able to make while I was a serving judge. All of them were written as occasional pieces, but they deal with questions which I hope have a significance extending well beyond the occasions which provoked them.

I have practised law, as an advocate and then a judge, for more than forty years. Lawyers participate in a process governed by formal rules designed to produce objective decision-making. But the process is not mechanical. It is intensely personal. There is a difference between an open mind and an empty mind. Very few judges approach questions of principle with a blank sheet of paper and work things out from first principles, as some philosophers claim to do. They usually start with hypotheses based on their own instincts, observations and experience, and test them until they find an answer which is more satisfactory (or less unsatisfactory) than any other. Their starting instincts and their personal observations and experience inevitably involve a bias towards certain kinds of solution. There are black-letter lawyers and lawyers who bring a greater measure of inventiveness to their task. There are activist lawyers and those who believe that the law should impose as little as possible on human affairs. There are instinctive believers in legal solutions and instinctive sceptics. The intensely deliberative nature of judicial decision-making, at any rate at the appellate level, usually irons out the grosser personal idiosyncracies. However, most of the problems with which lawyers have to deal are not about law at all. They are about fact and evidence. Lawyers are formed by experience to analyse complex factual issues in which they have no pre-existing expertise, often concerned with arcane scientific, economic or statistical concepts. It is a valuable discipline.

In spite of being a lawyer, I have never shaken off my origins as a professional historian, and never really wanted to. One result is that, as those who followed my 2019 Reith Lectures will know, I am sceptical about some things that other lawyers tend to take for granted. I am sceptical about the contribution that law has made to our public life, which many constitutional and administrative lawyers would regard as one of the law's crowning modern achievements. Law can resolve differences that would otherwise be resolved by violence, but I am sceptical of its ability to improve the lot of our society, let alone that of mankind at large. I doubt the value of multiplying rights, which often serve only to magnify and perpetuate grievances. I believe that litigation is an evil, a symptom of the breakdown of social norms. It is a necessary evil but an evil even so. Above all, I do not share the contempt that so many lawyers feel for the political process.

The strengths of the legal method at its best are objectivity, consistency, transparency and intellectual honesty. But in public affairs, these are not always virtues. Public life is too messy and human beings too idiosyncratic for that. Politics are not an unremitting search for truth. Their prime purpose is to enable people with conflicting opinions and interests to live together in peace. This necessarily entails untidy compromises and a measure of opacity and fudge. Sometimes we have to make space for the irrational because it has become too powerful an influence on our fellow citizens. Many of the conflicts with which politics are concerned cannot be analysed in purely rational terms. In some cases, instinct is not just the starting point for a process by which alternative hypotheses are tested. It is the guiding principle throughout. This has been a notable feature of the political scene in the past decade. Fear and insecurity, not reason or logic, dominated the arguments about Covid-19. Questions of identity have emerged as decisive in debates about immigration, Brexit and many other issues. This seems likely to be a lasting change, after many years in which such questions were swept aside. Perhaps the most fundamental question that we can ask about ourselves is Who are we? Is it a sufficient answer to say that we are human, or do we need some smaller category by which to identify ourselves? What is it to be English as opposed to Scottish, French or European? Are we in any meaningful sense the same people as those who once persecuted heretics or witches, or bought and sold slaves, or bombed Dresden? All of these are questions of identity. It pays to understand our past, because we are all in one way or another its prisoners. Those who study the past have many advantages – a vast fund of vicarious experience to broaden their outlook on human affairs and a ringside seat at the follies and delusions of mankind.

Inevitably, many of these essays touch on politically controversial issues. It is many years since I had any political allegiance. I have watched governments of different political complexions come and go with equal indifference. But no one should be indifferent to what happens in their society, and certainly I am not indifferent to what has been happening in mine over the past few years. Should an ex-judge be speaking about them at all? Judges have opinions like everyone else. As active, intelligent and observant citizens, how could they not? The convention, of which I whole-heartedly approve, is that serving judges do not allow their political opinions to be known. There are two principles at work here. First, judges should not make judicial decisions which properly belong to the world of politics. Second, they should not identify themselves with politically controversial positions that may undermine the perceived objectivity of their judicial decisions. It is their duty not just to put aside their personal political preferences when deciding cases, but to be seen to put them aside. None of these considerations is relevant to a former judge who is no longer making judicial decisions. I accept that one reason why people listen to me is that I was once a Supreme Court Judge, but that is not because they imagine that I am speaking judicially. I am now simply a citizen.

Jonathan Sumption
Greenwich, October 2020

HISTORY IN THE MODERN WORLD

THE HISTORIAN AS JUDGE

Forty years ago, I left my history fellowship at Magdalen College, Oxford, in order to become a barrister. I would like to be able to say that I was moved to do this by a thirst for justice in an imperfect world and a conviction that this was the best way that I could help my fellow citizens. Actually, my reasons were rather vulgar. I wanted to be able to pay my grocery bills, with perhaps a bit more left over than an academic salary could offer. Since then, I have thought of better reasons. But retrospective rationalisation should never be trusted, as I quickly discovered in my new profession.

I have never had any occasion to regret the decision. The law has paid my grocery bills. It has also left me with enough control over my own life to be able to continue my interest in historical scholarship. One of the shameful things about the current Research Assessment Framework for universities is that it makes it difficult for a professional academic to write a work of real substance. The emphasis on quantity rather than quality means that in order to sustain the finances of his or her department, an academic must have a regular output of published work. This means that the time available for research and writing tends to be consumed by the production of annual articles for peer-reviewed periodicals, which boost the department's research score without necessarily adding much to the sum of human understanding. A distinguished academic historian pointed out, in a review of my most recent volume on the Hundred Years War, that it was only by leaving the pressures of academic life for the presumably less pressured environment of the law that I had been able to write a work of historical scholarship on that scale. This idea provoked some hilarity among my friends. But actually the reviewer was not far from the truth.

Intellectually, the change from academic history to law was less of a jolt than I had expected. The study of the common law is an intensely historical process. Like any system of customary law dependent mainly on precedent, it is based on judicial decisions about the legal implications of a large number of tiny human stories. One could, of course, view these stories in the abstract, as if they were intellectual exercises written for a moot or a professional examination. But that would deprive them of much of their interest as well as of their poetry and their humanity. They are legal cautionary tales. But they are also accidental fragments of English history. As sources of law, they are completely different from the written codes that provide the basis of judicial decision-making in civil law countries. The French civil code originated in a deliberate attempt by Napoleon's jurists to efface the social values of the pre-revolutionary past. The result was, and is, a document that achieves an almost total degree of intellectual abstraction. It could be the law of almost any country on earth. Indeed, it is the law of quite a lot of countries on earth, having been adopted with minor variants in many places that have few cultural or historic connections with France. By comparison, the sources of English law could not have originated anywhere but England. They reflect the intense humanity of English law, something that makes its study both fascinating and enjoyable.

During my time on the Supreme Court I, like most of my colleagues, have been much exercised by the legal implications of British military operations in Iraq and Afghanistan.

The case law on this subject is like a precis of the history of British foreign policy over four centuries. It includes decisions about the Anglo-Danish trade wars of the seventeenth century, the depredations of the East India Company, to which Edmund Burke devoted some of his greatest parliamentary speeches, the ill-fated British occupation of Buenos Aires in 1806, the role of British mercenaries in the Portuguese civil wars of the 1830s, the forcible suppression of the West African slave trade by the Royal Navy, the scramble for African colonies at the end of the nineteenth century, the Jameson Raid and British interventions in Cyprus in the 1960s. And not only English history. There are also insights into the revolutions of 1830 in Germany, the civil wars of Venezuela and Mexico at the end of the nineteenth century and some of the more brutal incidents of the Russian Revolution.

This is, of course, an extreme example. One does not usually turn to law reports for stories of adventure or high politics. But even the placid ponds of the pre-1875 Chancery Division produced nuggets of historical gold, and sometimes more than nuggets. Much of the law of land tenure, conveyancing and trusts is unique to England and to those countries that have adopted English law. It reflects the preoccupations of the eighteenth- and nineteenth-century English aristocracy, the main purpose of which was to preserve their family line and its association with particular places, and above all with particular houses and pieces of land. Today, these considerations have lost almost all their former significance. But the basic principles of a system created in the very different social world of our ancestors still provides the framework of this area of law. One could make a very similar point about the law of undue influence, which seeks to save women and young people from the consequences of unwise transactions into which they were pushed, usually by overbearing relatives or manipulative religious mentors.

This branch of the law originated in a patriarchal society very different from the one in which we now live. It also owes much to a very Protestant suspicion of all religious enthusiasm. We are no longer very Protestant or all that patriarchal. But the law of undue influence is still with us. One of the best ways of understanding the law in these areas is to read Sir John Habakkuk's remarkable Ford Lectures of 1985, *Marriage, Debt and the Estates System, 1650–1850*. But for those who cannot face 800 pages of social history, however well written, the novels of Jane Austen and Anthony Trollope are a very adequate substitute. *Pride and Prejudice* is in a sense a prolonged commentary on the law of entailed land, with just enough fantasy to allow for a happy ending. Elizabeth Bennet had too small a marriage portion to hope for a good match, but still ended up by marrying the fabulously rich Darcy. In real life she would probably have been glad to make do with Mr Collins.

I have always found it difficult to resist turning to standard reference books such as the *Dictionary of National Biography* or the old *Cambridge Modern History*, in order to fill out the details of the older reported cases. Law reporters are austere fellows, and most of them are rather spare with detail. There is an obscure decision of 1816, which I once cited in court about the interpretation of a life insurance policy. It tells you nothing about the circumstances of the deceased's demise apart from judicial hints that it was rather shady. You have to look up old newspaper obituaries to discover the curious but legally irrelevant fact that the deceased was struck over the head with a pewter pot while celebrating the defeat of Napoleon – in Paris of all places. *Portarlington v Soulby* (1833) is not the sort of case that every practitioner carries about in his mental library. It is about the enforceability of gambling debts. It is perhaps a symptom of the triviality of my mind that I found it fascinating that Lord Portarlington, in addition to being a feckless and unskilful gambler, had been cashiered from the army for arriving at the battle of Waterloo five hours late with two days growth of beard. As it turned out, this was not an entirely useless piece of information. It helped me as Counsel to retain the interest of the Appellate Committee of the House of Lords when taking them through one of the drier judgments of Lord Brougham. You might think that this is just self-indulgence and romanticism. If so, you would be half right, although you should never underestimate the importance of entertainment as a tool of advocacy, or the poetic element in any well-written judgment.

There are, however, a number of more fundamental points to be made.

The first is perhaps too obvious to be worth stating. The rationale of any rule of law, and particularly a long-standing rule of law, is not always self-evident. It helps to understand how, historically, it came about and in response to what perceived mischief. Depending on the answer, the rule may be inapplicable, or simply redundant. But even if it is neither, it will at least be easier to understand. A good example is provided by two recent cases, *Crawford Adjusters v Sagicor* in the Privy Council and *Willers v Joyce* in the Supreme Court. In both of them, the court had to consider whether there was a tort of maliciously commencing or conducting civil proceedings, analogous to the well-established tort of malicious criminal prosecution. Opinions were divided, but in both cases the majority thought that the alleged tort did indeed exist. I am not proposing to go into the details of that argument, especially as I was in the minority in both cases. The point that I want to make about these cases is that it was necessary for us to ask ourselves why there appeared to be, in the existing authorities, a distinction between civil and criminal litigation. And whether such a distinction was justifiable today. These are difficult questions to answer without going back into some rather arcane aspects of English social history which explain why a tort of malicious criminal prosecution existed: the use of the law courts by litigants as a tool of oppression and an instrument of vendetta in the late middle ages, which led to the invention of a number of new torts; and the problems of public order in seventeenth- and eighteenth-century England, a society with no organised police force or system of public prosecution. Of course, a simpler way of approaching a question like that would have been to forget the history and proceed straight to the last stage of the inquiry. Never mind what happened in the fifteenth or the eighteenth century. What does justice require now? Ultimately, of course, that is the question that one does ask. But in a customary system of law like ours, it cannot be answered without reference to what earlier generations of judges have thought and said about it. The baggage of the past is always with us. Courts cannot ignore authority by which they are bound. Even the Supreme Court cannot approach the law of tort as if Britain were an uninhabited island awaiting its lawgiver, instead of a complex society shaped by a long past.

What this example illustrates is that it may be necessary to understand the historical background against which past cases were decided in order to ascertain what the law is. But there is more to it than that. A lawyer requires many skills. Knowing the law is only one of them, and not necessarily the most difficult. Among the others, perhaps the most important is an ability to weigh evidence and to analyse facts. Most litigation depends entirely on fact and not on law at all, except perhaps for a few basic and indisputable propositions. Even when there is a real issue of law, it will usually be found to turn on the correct classification of the facts. The more arcane the facts, the more valuable it is to have some background knowledge of the kind of conditions that produced them. I can think of few better illustrations than the work of an immigration and asylum judge. People who leave their homes and friends to seek a new life in a new and unfamiliar part of the world do not do so casually. Most of them are propelled by grinding poverty, personal misfortune, political crisis, persecution or natural disaster. Even economic migration is, I suspect, a portmanteau term for a complex bundle of motives. To comfortable and secure Englishmen, this is an alien world. I cannot speak from experience, but I would expect that a feel for the social world from which these people come is essential if one is to decide what the facts of their cases are likely to be. It is just one illustration, although quite an important one, of the value of a grasp of history and its methods for the practice of law, whether as an advocate or a judge.

Until relatively modern times all this would have been regarded as a truism. Let me take you back to the origins of the Oxford law faculty in the nineteenth century, another alien world, but one in which these questions were much discussed. At Oxford, a proper undergraduate school of English common law did not exist until 1850, although civil law had been taught there for centuries. However, for the first twenty-two years of its existence it was not an independent faculty. It was a joint school with modern history. The joint school provoked many questions about the value of history to a lawyer. The general opinion was that you could not be a good lawyer without a proper grasp of history. The first Chichele Professor of Modern History, Montague Burrows, delivering his inaugural lecture in 1862, told his audience that the object of the combined school was to 'form the judicial mind for the purpose of dealing in the best manner with all the problems of thought and practical life'. William Stubbs, the Regius Professor of History and perhaps the most influential Oxford historian ever, regarded the study of history as indispensable to a profession founded on the exercise of sound judgment. Historical enquiry, he once said, was an 'endless series of courts of appeal, ever ready to reopen closed cases'. The great medievalist John Horace Round had a rather different take on it. The problem with lawyers, he thought, was that they were too respectful of authority. Their vision was 'bounded by their books', whereas the historian was trained to question authority and to work from first principles. Acquaintance with the historical method could only be good for them. There is, I am afraid, something in Round's view, even now. He eventually concluded that lawyers were incorrigible and pressed for them to be allowed to go their own way, with their own faculty. That is what eventually happened in 1872. But many people regretted the separation, including at least two of the university's four law professors. Professors Maine and Holland told a Royal Commission a few years later that they regretted the creation of a separate school of law, giving substantially the same reasons for their opinion as Burrows and Stubbs.

After 1872, most would-be lawyers have voted with their feet. Judging by the sample whose careers I have been able to trace, in 1914 the great majority of the English judiciary, High Court and above, had degrees in classics, with history coming a distant second and law a long way behind. Fast forward to 1939 and the picture has hardly changed. It is only comparatively recently that a majority of practising lawyers have had law degrees. Even now, it is not universal in England as it is in many continental countries. I do not think that it was an accident that Tom Bingham, one of the great judges of the past century, read history at university and was an avid reader of history all his life. His interest in history unmistakably marked his style in both his judicial and his extra-judicial pronouncements. It also profoundly affected his approach to social problems. Of course, you can know a great deal of history without having studied it at university if you really set your mind to it. But however it is acquired, I have no doubt that a grasp of the dynamic of human societies through their history makes for a better judge. More generally, I would say that it improves the quality of almost every kind of decision-making. If President Woodrow Wilson had been a better historian when he set the agenda of the Versailles peace conference after the First World War, I doubt whether eastern Europe would have suffered the disasters that engulfed it in the two decades that followed. It can fairly be said that in the past half-century, British foreign policy has been somewhat accident-prone. Can this be something to do with the fact that the last prime ministers with a profound grasp of history were Harold Macmillan and Alec Douglas-Home?

We are, increasingly, a historically illiterate nation. Periodic opinion polls show that many of our fellow citizens have difficulty in saying in what century the Norman Conquest and even the Second World War occurred. A generation of children has been brought up on a remarkably narrow historical syllabus, essentially confined to the first half of the twentieth century, which is probably the most uncharacteristic century of Europe's past and unquestionably the most uncharacteristic century of Germany's. It offers very little insight into the way that societies develop over time. The result is to distort our understanding not just of history but of humanity itself. It also generates expectations of rapid change which all historical experience shows to be unrealistic. Many of the problems that confront a modern judge reflect these collective limitations.

It is permissible to regret the growing tendency of would-be lawyers to devote themselves only to the study of law from the age of eighteen. The law is an exclusive and possessive discipline, a priestly craft. But its study is not a particularly good training for the handling of evidence, or for acute social observation, or for the exercise of analytical judgement about facts, all of which are essential judicial skills. I am not for a moment suggesting that law graduates lack these qualities. But they do not derive them from their legal studies. I would also suggest that for those set upon a legal career, the study of a different subject at a formative time of one's life is personally enriching. It is a source of intellectual satisfaction, whatever contribution it may or may not make to one's subsequent professional life. Certainly, I have found it so. Over the years, I have made a great many enemies in law faculties up and down the land by suggesting that law should be offered only as a second degree, as it is in North America. I would not press this point today, for I doubt whether it is realistic, given the limited public funding available for extended study at university. But in an ideal world there would be much to be said for it.

There is, I think, a broader sense in which history supports a judge's role. It is a prodigious source of vicarious experience. We are all familiar with the tired journalistic cliché that judges are out of touch with real life because they are middle class and, by the standards of our society, comfortably off. The truth is that the cliché applies not just to lawyers but to everyone. Everybody is out of touch with real life. This is because real life is too vast and too varied for more than a small part of it to be experienced by any one man or woman. We need several lives, but we are granted only one. This is not just a problem peculiar to judges. It is as true of the noble lord who rules the state as it is of the noble lord who cleans his plate, or the aristocrat who banks at Coutts and the aristocrat who cleans his boots. In the nature of things, most experience is vicarious, not personal. History enables us to understand many things about humankind that we cannot hope to experience personally. Of course, its value would be very limited if we were all that different from our ancestors. But one of the things that one learns from our three millennia of recorded history is that humanity does not really change very much. What changes is not its basic instincts and desires but its capacity for giving effect to them. Indeed, one of the abiding tragedies of mankind is surely that its technical and organisational capacities have expanded so much faster than its social or moral sensibilities.

One of the most interesting sources that I use for my work as a historian is the French chancery registers of the late middle ages. Several hundred volumes of them sit in the Archives Nationales in Paris. They consist mainly of pardons. In these fascinating documents, one has little potted biographies of tens of thousands of late medieval criminals, almost all of them poor wretches who for one reason or another had found themselves on the wrong side of life's chances. I met many of these people during the twelve years that I sat as a part-time Recorder in London Crown Courts. The accounts of their doings and the assessments of their culpability read exactly like the social enquiry reports prepared for sentencing hearings. At the opposite end of the social scale, the ambitions and activities of courtiers and officials are remarkably like those of dealers and managers in modern investment banking houses. There really is nothing new under the sun.

By the admittedly narrow standards of modern professional life, the bar and the bench are surprisingly varied groups of people. There are, I believe, no longer ex-policemen and ex-merchant seamen at the bar, as there once were. But among the sample of barristers and judges of whom I have some knowledge, I can count a former actor, a concert pianist, a doctor, a chemist, and several accountants, merchant bankers and surveyors, as well as a number of refugees from academic life in disciplines other than law. It may be that someone else will speak about 'the concert pianist as judge'. I am by no means unusual in having once done something else, and I am certainly not unique in continuing to do it in tandem with the law. It has enriched my life. I hope that it has made me better at both things.

This talk was originally delivered on 6 October 2016 in the Rolls Building of the High Court. The audience consisted of judges of the Upper Tribunal, who hear appeals from the decisions of specialised tribunals, generally about administrative decisions of government services, including immigration appeals.

2

ON APOLOGISING FOR HISTORY

In June 1997, Britain's newly appointed prime minister, Tony Blair, apologised for the Irish potato famine of 1846 in a letter read out to an Irish audience at a public meeting in Cork. He was much praised for this act at the time. It struck the note of humility that is increasingly admired in our politicians. But the question which occurred to me when his gesture was reported in the press was a more fundamental one: what did his apology actually mean?

It is a question worth asking. The tide of public apology for historic wrongs grows stronger by the year. It has been estimated by a reputable authority that Pope John Paul II apologised in public on at least ninety-four occasions for the misdeeds of the Christian past. There have been energetic campaigns to obtain apologies from the Turks for the Armenian massacres of 1915–16; from the Japanese for their wars in the Far East in the 1930s and 1940s; and from the British for the bombing of Dresden during the Second World War. Ought there to be an apology for the Atlantic slave trade that flourished from the sixteenth century to the nineteenth? If so, who should do the apologising? And to whom? Would it help? And, if so, why?

It is now nearly ninety years since Herbert Butterfield protested, in a famous book,[1] against the prevailing tendency to see the past in terms of current issues. This is a battle that Butterfield has comprehensively lost. The number of modern apologies for the horrors of the past is perhaps the ultimate symptom of his defeat. It is essentially a rebuke to the past for not being more like the present. It marginalises historical events by treating them as monstrous aberrations from a path of truth chosen by our own generation. This is not just intellectually impure. It obstructs our understanding of the past. In the process it deprives us of a great fund of vicarious experience that history might otherwise have opened up to us. If we simply reject the past without trying to understand it, we are unlikely to learn from it.

Let us return for a moment to the papacy. I am not a Catholic, but I regard the papacy as a particularly interesting case. It is probably the most ancient political institution on the planet with a continuous existence up to our own day. It has been there for at least sixteen centuries in something like its present form. During those centuries, humanity has experienced much, and its values have undergone great changes. No one, I imagine, would question the appropriateness of the present Pope apologising for the recent wrongs, such as the abuse of children in Catholic schools and orphanages. These things were contrary to what the Church has always taught and every civilised society has always believed. There are victims still alive to remember the abuse and acknowledge the apology. But what are we to say about John Paul II's apology in March 2000 for the Christian wars and persecutions of the middle ages? The world would probably be a better place today if these things had never happened. We should certainly not behave in the same way now, although we sometimes do. But these are rather banal sentiments, and the Pope was presumably trying to say more than that. How much more was he saying? Was he saying that medieval crusaders and inquisitors ought to have taken the same view in their own day about the morality of religious violence as he himself did at the dawn of the twenty-first century? If so, why should they have taken that view, and on the basis of what values and what experience? He might as well have criticised his predecessors for failing to master the principles of double-entry book-keeping or the psychological theories of Becker and Jung.

The justification usually advanced for historic apology is a simple and pragmatic one. It may serve to heal a still-open sore. It is a small price to pay for the comfort that it may bring to those who identify themselves with the victims. Applying the utilitarian calculus, is it not better to cultivate their goodwill than that of the odd historical purist like me? My own answer to this would be that apologising for the past is not just a historical anachronism. There are also serious philosophical and moral objections to it. It does not even satisfy the utilitarian calculus.

The philosophical objection is this. When we castigate the sins of our forebears as immoral, we are saying, implicitly, that there are some moral principles that are absolute and eternal, not relative and ephemeral, by which men may justly be condemned in any age. The difficulty about that, as Adam Smith pointed out long ago in his *Theory of Moral Sentiments*, is that if there are eternal moral values independent of the changing understanding and sentiments of humans, then there must be some source for them other than humans themselves. In other words, there must be some external and authoritative revelation. But revelation is not a very useful tool for conducting a discourse between generations separated by a gulf of understanding several centuries wide. It was, of course, in the name of revelation that men joined the armies of the crusades, or organised pogroms against the medieval Jews. It was in the name of revealed truth that churchmen persecuted Galileo and condemned the teachings of Harvey and Darwin. Surely we can do better than that today.

What is morally objectionable about the practice of apologising for these wrongs now, is that it depends upon a concept of collective and inherited guilt which is indefensible. As it happens, the most famous illustration of the concept of transmitted guilt is also one of the most manifestly wicked. The justification advanced in the first sixteen centuries of European Christianity for the persecution of the Jews was that they had a collective and inherited responsibility for the death of Christ. All of us would today reject this notion as absurd. But is it any more respectable when applied to other historical injustices?

On the day after Pope John Paul's homily of March 2000, an Italian bishop was asked for his reaction. He replied with a question of his own: 'In whose name, exactly, is the Holy Father asking pardon?' He was making a fair point. When we ask a public figure for an apology for some historic wrong, we presumably expect more than mere hand-wringing regret for the sins of humanity. We expect him to speak for some specific section of humanity that can be regarded as accepting responsibility. This requires some institutional continuity. There is no one today with the institutional status to apologise for that unprovoked act of international aggression, the Norman conquest of England. A statement from the Prefect of Seine-Atlantique would hardly do. By comparison, John Paul II's words had some resonance because he was speaking as the institutional leader of all Catholics and the successor of the medieval popes who had preached the crusade and founded the Inquisition. This is presumably why he said that he was apologising for the past sins of *Catholics*. But as a matter of moral judgment, one might ask: Why just Catholics? Do not Protestants also belong to communities that were once associated with the crusades, the Inquisition and the persecution of the Jews? Of course they do. The only difference is that the Pope cannot speak for them.

It is worth asking on what basis the Pope can speak even for Catholics on such an issue. When Tony Blair apologised for the Irish potato famine in 1997, he was, I suppose, doing so as the institutional successor of the prime minister of the time, Sir Robert Peel. Yet he was plainly not speaking for the English political community of the 1840s, to whom Peel had been answerable. He was speaking for me, for you, and for all of us. By what right was he doing that? The Irish potato famine was not only a great human tragedy, but a political catastrophe the impact of which on Anglo-Irish relations was poisonous for both countries. But an apology says more than that. It seeks to engage my moral responsibility. Yet in what sense am I responsible? I am descended from nineteenth-century Englishmen. I live in the same country as they did, speaking the same language. Yet I did not do it. You did not do it. It was not done on our behalf.

That brings me to the position of the victims. They, too, are long since dead. Yet, just as there has to be someone who can represent the original perpetrator, so there has to be someone to apologise to, some individual or group that can be said to represent the ancient victims. Here we are confronted by an even greater artifice. Consider, for example, the demands for a public apology for the eighteenth-century slave trade. Its victims suffered terrible hardship and injustice. The injury done to them by the slavers, and perhaps by the societies that tolerated such things, is obvious. But the suggestion is that the apology is due to the dispersed descendants of the original slaves who are alive today. It is not obvious what injury has been done to them. Many of them enjoy better lives in the countries to which their ancestors were forcibly deported than they would have enjoyed if their families had remained in sub-Saharan Africa. In what sense, other than a purely genealogical one, do they represent the victims of the original wrong?

We apologise in order to be forgiven. It is a two-way process, comprising contrition on one side and the discarding of resentment on the other. When I apologise for treading on someone's toe or losing my temper with them, I am recognising my fault, promising not to do it again and asking them in some measure to absolve me. But who is in a position to grant absolution for the sins that our ancestors committed against a long-dead generation? To promote forgiveness in these circumstances, you have to create an entirely artificial class of victims. It is an open question whether the political apologies of the last two decades have in fact promoted harmony in our own world, even according to the utilitarian calculus. It is at least as likely that by accepting the practice of political apology for the past, we simply perpetuate the sense of grievance by making it heritable. It seems obvious that this has been one result of the campaign for Turkish recognition of the Armenian massacres of 1915. Would it really increase the sum of human happiness if the prime minister of Turkey now came forward to apologise for these terrible events on behalf of a generation that has grown up since, and a Turkey that is not even the same state? I doubt it.

It is of course the very fact that such appalling historical tragedies happened before our time, to people long since dead, that makes it so easy to apologise for them. The passage of time makes the moral quandaries of the past seem so much simpler than they were at the time. Take the German occupation of France and the connivance of the Vichy government in its crimes. These events presented many Frenchmen with unspeakable dilemmas between 1940 and 1944. At what point do passivity and compliance in the face of brute strength shade into collaboration? It is probably an unanswerable question. In the aftermath of the war a whole generation of Frenchmen declined to ask it. It was only in the late 1970s that a later generation, which had never had to face the same quandaries, found it morally straightforward to distribute blame. Much the same can be said of the rising tide of moral disapproval of the wartime bombing of Dresden and other German cities by the British and American air forces. War is by definition a breakdown in civilised values. It is not easy for a democracy to compute the right or proportionate response to an unprovoked war unleashed against it by a powerful and savage enemy. Germany was a defeated nation in February 1945, but had refused to recognise the fact, and was fighting on at great cost to its own and Allied lives. Yet these problems are not sufficiently recognised in *Der Brand*, Jorg Friedrich's scholarly best-seller on the Allied bombing of German cities or even in A. C. Grayling's more cautious and thoughtful work *Among the Dead Cities*, books which have set the tone for our modern revulsion against the acts of our parents' generation. What these works show is that the misdeeds of our ancestors still resonate, long after their moral dilemmas have been forgotten. By comparison, we experience our own dilemmas directly. They still have the power to reduce us to silence.

In May 2020, George Floyd, a Black American man, was killed by a policeman in Minneapolis during an arrest, after supposedly passing a forged $20 bill in a shop. The policeman knelt on his neck for eight minutes, preventing him from breathing, until he died. This shocking event prompted a worldwide outbreak of anger. It was directed not just against police forces in the United States, where unfortunately such events are not uncommon, but also against the degrading treatment of Black people everywhere. And not only against their degrading treatment now, but against their degrading treatment in the past. In Britain, a statue of Edward Colston in Bristol was pulled down and dumped in the river by demonstrators. Colston was a Bristol merchant and Member of Parliament who died three hundred years ago. Between

21

1680 and 1692, he was a shareholder of the Royal African Company, a chartered company which until 1689 had a monopoly of the English slave trade from West Africa to the Caribbean and the Americas. By the standards of Colston's own day, this was a respectable trade. King Charles II was the honorary governor of the company. The future King James II was an active director. Other investors included the philosopher John Locke and the diarist Samuel Pepys. After severing his connection with the Royal Africa Company, Colston conducted a modest trade in slaves for his own account until 1708, when he retired to his estates. When he died in 1721 he left his fortune to trustees to found various charities in Bristol, including almshouses, hospitals and schools. A similar fate has befallen the great London philanthropist Sir John Cass, another shareholder of the Royal Africa Company. His foundation is now apparently to be renamed after three centuries of charitable activity in the City. His statue is to be removed from the façade of its headquarters. In the same spirit, Edinburgh University has posthumously disavowed David Hume, its greatest alumnus and one of the greatest British philosophers, on the ground that he once lent money to a friend to buy slaves.

The example of the statue wreckers of Bristol has been widely followed. Demands have been made for the renaming of streets and the removal of statues commemorating not just those who themselves engaged in the slave trade but others who were descended from those who did, such as the great Victorian prime ministers Sir Robert Peel and William Gladstone. The tide of retrospective anger has spread to embrace imperialists such as Robert Clive, whose military victories laid the foundation of the British Empire in India; the businessman Cecil Rhodes, who made millions out of mining in South Africa and was one of the leading figures in the expansion of the British Empire across sub-Saharan

Africa; and military heroes who fought in Britain's many
colonial wars or had been colonial administrators, such as
Wellington, who was commander-in-chief in India, and the
great Victorian hero Sir Henry Havelock, who recaptured
Lucknow during the Indian Mutiny.

The objection to this rage against the past is essentially
the same as the objection to historical apologies. It seeks to
remove memorials of the past because the past did not share
the values of the present. This is an irrational and absurd
thing to do. What has happened has happened. It will not
unhappen, however angry we are about it. The wealth that
Colston and Cass derived from the slave trade will still be
used to pay for the charities that they founded, whether they
are named after them or not. David Hume will continue to
be read and admired as a philosopher whether or not Edinburgh University acknowledges him. No sensible person
would suggest that the existence of statues honouring their
contributions to British life makes us think well of the slave
trade today. The most that can be said about them is that
their existence shows that there was once a time when people
did not feel as strongly about slavery as we do now. But, so
what? Very few of the values that we hold dear today were
equally admired by our ancestors. Historically, most societies
have abhorred democracy, rejected religious and political
tolerance and regarded the whole idea of racial or gender
equality as ridiculous. Are we to pretend that the past did not
exist? It is said that public monuments should commemorate
only those who share our values. Are we really so obsessed
with ourselves that we wish to efface every public reminder
that people once thought differently? And to what end? Such
demonstrations serve no purpose other than the emotionally self-indulgent purpose of advertising the strength of the
demonstrator's feelings.

They are also in an important sense an attack on

humanity itself. Human societies are the product of their past. They have never been wholly good or wholly bad in any age. Slavery supplied the material foundation of the civilisations of both Greece and Rome. Yet Greece and Rome are the ultimate sources of many of the fundamental values of our own world and have bequeathed to us works of art of inspiring beauty and literature of great profundity. Britain's merchants played a leading part in the eighteenth-century slave trade, but its courts, government and navy also played a leading part in its suppression in the nineteenth. The British colonial empire had dark moments, but bright ones as well. On the whole, it was a benign force in an age when European civilisation and traditions of government had much to offer other continents. Of course, that is a matter of opinion and there is room for disagreement about it. But to present what was bad about our past as if it was the whole is to falsify history. The mixture of darkness and light is an essential part of the process by which human societies have developed into what they are now. We learn from the mistakes and iniquities of our forebears as well as celebrating their achievements. Action and reaction are the basic mechanism of progress. And so it is with philanthropists like Colston and Cass or philosophers like David Hume. That they had links with the slave trade is an important fact about them. But the movement to get rid of their statues or rename their institutions is based on the idea that nothing else about them matters. So it casts aside statues that were erected to honour their philanthropy or their philosophy, not their slave trading. This is obsessive and fanatical, characteristics that we would not admire in any other context. It also rejects what is wonderful and fascinating about humanity, in favour of a monochrome view of the past which is both misleading and philistine.

In the end, the approach of the historian, however pedantic and morally pinched it may seem, is surely right. History is morally neutral. We have a duty to understand why things happened as they did, but apologising for them or trying to efface them is morally worthless. It gets in the way of understanding. Once the relevant actors have left the scene, there is no longer a live moral issue, no longer a perpetrator to be contrite or a victim to forgive. For those left behind, there are only lessons to be learned.

This piece began life as a talk to the salon held every other month by Oliver Black and Edmund Fawcett in Oliver's unusual home in Elder Street, near Liverpool Station. For years before Oliver Black's tragic death in 2019 these salons were occasions for civilised discussion of an eclectic range of historical, scientific and philosophical issues. This talk was originally delivered there early in 2011 and then, in substantially the same form, the following May, as a contribution to the BBC's Fore Thought series. I have updated it to cover the most recent outbreak of rage against the past, following from the Black Lives Matter movement.

3

MAGNA CARTA THEN AND NOW

It is impossible to say anything new about Magna Carta, unless you say something mad. In fact, even if you say something mad, the likelihood is that it will have been said before, probably quite recently. Historically, there have been two schools of thought about this famous charter. The first can conveniently be called the lawyer's view, although it is held by many people who are not lawyers. This holds the charter to be a major constitutional document, the foundation of the rule of law and the liberty of the subject in England. The other is the historian's view, which has tended to emphasise the self-interested motives of the barons and has generally been sceptical about the charter's constitutional significance.

There are obvious reasons why lawyers should have taken the lead in extolling Magna Carta. There have been periods in our history when law has acquired an intensely ideological flavour. One of them was the first half of the seventeenth century, when lawyers provided much of the leadership of the parliamentary opposition to Charles I, and the law courts themselves became an important political battleground between absolute and limited monarchy. Another is our own age, in which government is once again held in low regard and law is invoked as a source of nobler, more liberal and more principled values than mere politics.

Lawyers have, on the whole, been bad historians. This is

because with a few honourable exceptions they have treated the history of law as a self-contained and self-sufficient discipline based almost exclusively on the study of legal texts. They have been much less interested in the social and cultural context in which law is made. Yet, like any system of customary law, English law has adapted itself to reflect the values of each successive generation. Manifestly, the values of the early thirteenth century were not the same as our own. The chief sinner, and by far the most influential, was Sir Edward Coke, one of the leading opponents of the early Stuart kings and the man who more than any other individual was responsible for inventing the myth of Magna Carta. I shall return to this interesting and rebarbative figure below. At this stage I simply draw attention to Coke's principal defect as a historian. He was only interested in legal sources: charters, statutes and the year-books that served as the law reports of the middle ages. He read them entirely without regard to their context, as if they had been addressed to seventeenth-century gentlemen like himself. He did not think that there was any point in understanding the mentality of those who wrote them, which he assumed to be the same as his own. It never occurred to him that legal historians had anything to learn from the chronicles and political records of the past. His advice to general historians was to keep out. 'Let them meddle not with any point or secret of any art or science, especially with the laws of this realm,' he wrote.

Historians were once content to adopt the myths of the lawyers. It suited the patriotic view of English exceptionalism, which was for many years the stuff of historical writing in England. It was not until the beginning of the twentieth century that historians dared to suggest a more sceptical view. In 1904 Edward Jenks, an Oxford academic lawyer, published a famous article entitled 'The myth of Magna Carta'. This was followed the next year by W. S. McKechnie's *Magna*

Carta. McKechnie was, like Jenks, an academic lawyer. He was a Scottish solicitor and a lecturer in constitutional law at Glasgow University. But Jenks and McKechnie were also formidable general historians. McKechnie in particular subjected the charter to a minute and immensely learned exegesis, for the first time putting each of its clauses into their historical context and in the process exposing a number of misconceptions. His theme was taken up by Maurice Powicke, the future Regius Professor of History at Oxford, in a distinguished contribution to a collection of essays published to mark the last centenary of Magna Carta in 1915.

There is no doubt that the lawyers have been more successful in propagating their views than the historians. Maitland, the great Victorian historian of English law, set the tone by declaring Magna Carta to be a 'sacred text'. It was, he wrote, 'the nearest approach to an unrepealable fundamental statute that England had ever had', even though much of it had in fact already been repealed at the time he wrote these words. These sentiments persist into our own day, and have been uncritically adopted by politicians and journalists. In her famous, or if you prefer infamous speech at Bruges in 1988, Mrs Thatcher referred to the charter as the origin of representative government. A subsequent tenant of Downing Street, David Cameron, armed with a copy of an Edwardian illustrated text-book for children, called it the document that paved the way for democracy, equality and the rule of law, the 'foundation of all our laws and liberties'. The current prime minister, Boris Johnson, has called it 'the foundation document of freedom and constitutional government'. Now, I have nothing against the liberty of the subject, the rule of law, legal aid, democracy, motherhood or apple pie. But I do have a problem with the distortion of history to serve an essentially modern political agenda. Claims such as those I have just cited are high-minded tosh. They represent the worst kind of ahistorical Whiggism. They encapsulate the view mocked a generation ago in a famous essay by Herbert Butterfield, that the past can be viewed as an accident-prone but on the whole persistent march towards the manifest rightness of our own values.

The first thing we need to do, if we are to appreciate the historical significance of Magna Carta, is to understand the world in which it was created. Contrary to common belief, the middle ages was not an age of absolute monarchy, either before or after Magna Carta. It never could have been. Medieval societies generated very small surpluses over and above the basic cost of subsistence. Governments therefore had limited resources of money and manpower. They could not govern without the tacit support of their subjects, and the active support of at least the most powerful of them. Medieval governments depended for their survival on an unstable mixture of sentiment, legitimacy and bluff, in the same way that most governments did until comparatively modern times. This meant that kings could not afford to act in a way that defied the contemporary consensus about how a king should behave. One of the key elements of that consensus was that the king should act in accordance with law.

The great English political theorist of the generation before Magna Carta was John of Salisbury, who wrote his major work, the *Policraticus*, in the 1150s. He believed that the difference between a king and a tyrant was that a king ruled by law. Kings, he taught, were subject to legal constraints that protected the liberty of the individual from arbitrary government. The king could not simply change these constraints at will. By comparison, a tyrant had no greater authority for his acts than physical force. I cite John of Salisbury not because his views were particularly original, but because they were entirely commonplace. He was the most articulate exponent in his time of the conventional view of the state. The barons at Runnymede had certainly not read the *Policraticus*. It is unlikely that they had even heard of it, although their spokesman Stephen Langton, Archbishop of Canterbury, probably had. But the middle ages was an intensely law-minded age, and the barons had a developed notion of fundamental law. They knew perfectly well that the king could not do as he liked, either in theory or in practice.

Where did this fundamental law come from? John of Salisbury answered this question by saying that it came from God. The baronage would have given a different answer. They would have said that it came from immemorial custom. In twelfth-century England, people spoke of the laws of King Edward the Confessor. Edward the Confessor reigned from 1042 to 1066. The exact content of his laws was a matter of some doubt. He is not known to have issued any code of laws, although various spurious codes bearing his name were written and circulated during the twelfth and thirteenth centuries. What people really meant by the laws of Edward the Confessor was not so much an ascertainable body of law, as an ideal state of law belonging to an imagined golden age before the Norman conquest. Medieval men were deeply pessimistic about the capacity of mankind to improve itself. They did not expect a progressive amelioration of the human condition, as we do. They looked for their golden age in the past, and saw history as a tale of the decline and corruption inseparable from human affairs. This is why medieval kings did not, as the Roman emperors had done, make law in the plenitude of their power. With the aid of counsellors and wise men, they derived it from the revelation of existing law, whose authority came from its antiquity. The most that could be done was to define it, to express it in better words. Their view could not have been more different from our modern assumption that our destiny lies in our own hands and that the golden age lies ahead of us.

At the time of his coronation in 1100, Henry I swore an oath to observe the laws and customs of England. He defined what was meant by this in a famous charter in which he undertook to abstain from various illegal acts that had been practised by his predecessor, William Rufus. Rufus's practices, Henry said, had not been law. On the contrary, they had 'unjustly oppressed the law of England', and he (Henry) would correct this by restoring the laws of Edward the Confessor. Henry's successors also issued coronation charters, which were either directly modelled on Henry I's or simply confirmed it. These charters were in reality bids for their subjects' support, without which a newly crowned king could not govern. There is plenty of evidence in the records and chronicles of the period to show that people knew about these promises and sometimes justified resistance to the king's demands by reference to them. They regarded them as law. During the negotiations for Magna Carta, Stephen Langton produced Henry I's charter. The drafting of the final version of Magna Carta was based in part upon it.

So, it is true that Magna Carta stands for the rule of law. But it is not true that Magna Carta was the origin of the principle. The English kings had doubtless broken the law quite frequently before Magna Carta, and they continued to break it afterwards. But the idea that the king was subject to law had for a very long time been part of the orthodoxy of medieval constitutional thought both in England and elsewhere. The barons did not invent it at Runnymede. Their object was to define what the law was. No one doubted that whatever it was, the king was subject to it.

This, however, does not mean that twelfth-century Englishmen were constitutionalists before their time. The law which governed the king's relations with his lay subjects was of a very limited kind. It was closer in spirit to a private contract than a constitution. It was concerned almost entirely with the king's feudal rights and obligations. These rights and obligations related to the terms governing the holding of land at a time when land was the main source of wealth and the sole source of status apart from royal or ecclesiastical office. By virtue of his ultimate dominion over land, the king had an obligation to administer justice to his direct tenants (usually called 'tenants-in-chief'). He had a right to require them to serve in his courts and councils, and within limits to serve him in war. He had a right, for example, to take control of the lands of those who could not perform military service because they were minors or women. He was entitled to levy premiums known as 'fines' when heirs entered into their inheritance. He could levy a tax known as scutage in lieu of the vassal's obligations of military service. He could charge fees for litigation in his courts, which was the only way of establishing a contested title to land. These rights were matters of great moment to baronial families as well as to their own vassals who had a similar relationship with them. They critically affected the finances of landowners and their standing in society. But they had nothing to do with the machinery of government and were hardly the stuff of what we would now call constitutional law.

There is another problem about treating the various charters regulating feudal rights as a kind of precocious constitutionalism. There was no institutional mechanism for enforcing the king's obligations on him against his will. Magna Carta certainly did not provide one. The king's judges were the king's, in fact as well as in name. It would be several centuries before any recognisable concept of judicial independence emerged. And, although there was a general convention that the king should take the advice of his leading subjects, nothing recognisable as a representative parliament existed before the second half of the thirteenth century. The only remedy against abuse was defiance, a technical term for the formal renunciation of the feudal bond that was the sole source of the king's authority. Defiance released both parties from their obligations and legitimised rebellion. The outcome then became a matter of force, not law.

This is what happened in 1215. The essential problem of the Angevin kings of England was that there was no system of national taxation. Henry II, Richard and John, all fought expensive wars against domestic rebels, mainly in their French domains. They took advantage of the indefinite character of their feudal rights to extort money to fund the cost of warfare. For example, they disposed of wardships and heiresses, not for conventional sums but for whatever the market would bear, which was often a great deal. The husbands whom they found for them were likely to be rich, but were not always the ladies' cups of tea. They imposed heavy scutages in lieu of military service. They took advantage of their vassals' delinquencies to dispossess them. They withheld justice from those whom they regarded as having placed themselves beyond the law. John was no different in these respects from his brother and father. But his financial needs were greater, for he faced not just rebellion in his French dominions but a full-scale invasion of his French domains by Philip August, King of France. He therefore pressed his rights further than they had. A large faction within the baronage, mainly from the north of England, responded by defying him and waging war against him. They captured London and forced him to submit to their demands at Runnymede.

The framers of Magna Carta would be surprised to learn of their posthumous fame. Its title, the 'Great Charter', was only acquired later in the thirteenth century. Even then the title was not intended to refer to the greatness of its contents, but only to distinguish it from the smaller charter of the forest issued two years afterwards. Magna Carta, properly so-called, was a deeply conservative document. It sought to enforce on the king conventions that were profoundly traditional, and obligations that he and his predecessors had acknowledged for more than a century. There are no high-flown declarations of principle. No truths are held to be self-evident. Indeed, there are hardly any provisions that can be called constitutional at all. On the contrary, its contents are rather mundane. There are clauses to protect the interests of the barons and their chief allies, the Church and the City of London. These are followed by a large number of highly technical provisions about the feudal incidents of land tenure. They are all essentially about money. The charter is a long catalogue of the ways in which John and his brother and father had abused their rights as feudal superiors in order to extract money from their subjects. There was nothing new about any of this, except that the more indefinite obligations of the king were defined more exactly, for example by putting figures on what the king could charge by way of entry fines.

The charter was a classic appeal to legal tradition, combined with an attempt at definition which was all that contemporary sentiment expected of legislation. This is especially true of what is undoubtedly the most famous of Magna Carta's clauses, Articles 39 and 40:

> No free man shall be arrested or imprisoned, or dispossessed, or outlawed or exiled, or otherwise destroyed, nor will we proceed against him, or send others to do so, except by the lawful judgment of his peers or by the law of the land. To no one will we sell, or deny, or delay justice or right.

This was directed to a specific grievance of the barons against King John. It is a technical subject on which scholars are not agreed. In summary, since the 1160s, the king's justices had enjoyed exclusive jurisdiction over all disputes between free men about title to freehold land. But in the case of disputes between the king's tenants-in-chief, essentially the baronage and the richer knights, the king enjoyed a personal judicial competence that was inherent in his position as their immediate feudal superior. John had been in the habit of giving judgment personally in such cases, with only his lowly household knights and officers present instead of the great men who could ordinarily have expected to attend. There was a large political element in many of his decisions. He had unquestionably sold justice, by demanding large sums known as 'proffers' in return for access to his court. And on occasions he had denied justice. The baronage therefore found themselves squeezed. Their own tenants had unrestricted access to the king's justices for their claims, but they themselves were dependent on the vagaries of the king's will for their claims against him or each other. This was what Articles 39 and 40 were about. They imposed on the king himself the same standards of justice as were already required of his professional judges.

Certainly, Articles 39 and 40 were nothing to do with trial by jury. In 1215, juries had been used for certain special purposes for about half a century, but criminal trials were decided by ordeal or battle, not by the verdict of a jury. Juries only gradually came into use for criminal trial in the course of the thirteenth century, as a result of the prohibition by the Church on the clergy participating in these more primitive methods of finding facts. Nor were Articles 39 and 40 the origin of *habeas corpus*. This was developed by the king's courts long after Magna Carta, although writs to much the same effect had sometimes been issued under Henry II, half a century before. Article 39 prevented the arrest of a subject without legal authority, a swipe against King John's use of the machinery of the law to destroy his enemies. But this part of Article 39 was a weak reed, for it did not say what constituted legal authority. Every medieval and every Tudor king exercised a right of arrest, either personally or through his ministers, generally in order to incarcerate people for reasons of state. The king's warrant was regarded by the courts as a sufficient answer to a writ of *habeas corpus* until the seventeenth century.

So why do we single out Magna Carta as the origin of the rule of law? We might equally have celebrated the 800th anniversary of the coronation charters of Henry I, King Stephen or Henry II if we had thought of it in time. The answer is that what was special about it was not the ideas it embodied, which were perfectly conventional, but the dramatic circumstances in which it came into existence. Custom is by definition uncertain. It becomes certain only when it is challenged, so that its ambit can be tested. King John challenged his barons' view of the law and failed. His obligations were enforced against him. Moreover, they were enforced with a fanfare of spectacle and drama that could never be matched by a coronation charter or a legal treatise.

The life of the original Magna Carta was brief. Within ten weeks the Pope, Innocent III, denounced it as 'not only shameful and base but illegal and unjust'. He declared it to be null and void, and forbade the king to observe it on pain of excommunication. John died in October 1216 and was succeeded by his nine-year-old son, Henry III. Nothing could be permanently settled while he was a minor, and it was not until 1225 that the status of Magna Carta was finally resolved. In that year, Henry reissued the charter in a revised form. The new text left out a number of the provisions that imposed constitutional limitations on the king's power to govern. It left out Article 61 of the original text, which created a permanent council of twenty-five barons to enforce the charter on the king. It left out the provisions of Articles 12 and 14 which prevented the king from levying taxation unless by the 'common counsel of the realm'. In other words it left out anything which might have created an alternative source of constitutional authority able to challenge the king. According to the Barnwell chronicle, the king conceded the revised Magna Carta *'benigne et hilariter'*, graciously and cheerfully. In return, the baronage consented to a heavy new tax. Taxpayers were told that unless they paid they would not enjoy the liberties that the king had conceded. Copies were distributed throughout England, to the counties and the larger towns. When, later in the thirteenth century, the charter was formally confirmed by Henry III and his son Edward I, it was in the version of 1225. It was this text that was recorded on the statute rolls as the authentic instrument, not the earlier versions.

Between 1258 and 1265, there was a prolonged baronial rebellion against Henry III. The barons justified this step by reference to Magna Carta. They claimed that Henry III had acted against the terms of the charter by oppressing the Church, despoiling heirs and disparaging heiresses, and so on. In particular he had exploited the feudal rights of the Crown to raise money without consent. In other words, their basic grievances were the same as they had been under King John. They were complaining about the abuse of the king's feudal rights for financial gain. Their problem was that there was no way of making him observe the charter in these respects without imposing some kind of permanent control over his government. The Provisions of Oxford, which were imposed on Henry III in 1258, therefore took the government of the kingdom out of his hands by creating a council drawn from the ranks of the baronage, on whose advice he was bound to act. They did this in the name of the rule of law. The *Song of Lewes*, the famous Latin poem of 1264, which expressed the rebels' ideas, put it very pithily: *'Lex stat, rex cadit'* ('Let the law stand, though the king falls'). The baronial rebellion against Henry III exposed the weakness of Magna Carta, which was that it was not a constitutional document but merely a code of feudal law. The problem was that far from it being a blueprint for future constitutional development, Magna Carta was really the last gasp of the old order that was passing away.

In the three centuries that followed the scene at Runnymede, changes occurred in English society which made the sort of issues that the charter dealt with less important. In the first place, Magna Carta had been directed mainly to protecting the financial interests of tenants-in-chief, a very small group of perhaps 150 to 180 men. It provided for tenants-in-chief to make the same rights available to their own feudal subordinates. Only the unfree, the tied peasants who constituted perhaps half the population of England, were left out. But with the prolonged agricultural boom of the thirteenth century, the rapid increase of England's population, the expansion of the cash economy, and the growing turnover of land, these categories became increasingly meaningless. The traditional feudal hierarchy no longer provided a mechanism for the exercise of power. Second, lawyers invented ways of evading the more burdensome obligations associated with feudal tenure. This applied particularly to the rights of the Crown that arose on the transmission of property to a man's heirs, which had been at the heart of the disputes between King John and the barons. The lawyers' most fertile invention was the 'use', or trust, which they devised at the end of the thirteenth century and which became extremely popular with landowners over the next two hundred years. The use worked by vesting the property in a continuing body of trustees, so that the landowner never died. Third, the kings no longer depended on feudal obligation to recruit their armies. The last English king to make extensive use of the feudal military obligation was Edward I, who died in 1307. The last summons of feudal host was in 1327. From the middle of the fourteenth century, the wars of the kings of England were fought by volunteers who served for honour and wages. Their obligations were based on contract and on money payment, not on the tenure of land. Increasingly, soldiering became a professional career, whose connections with the structure of English society were casual and accidental.

Finally, and perhaps most important of all, the creation of representative parliaments in the second half of the thirteenth century put the dealings between the king and his subjects on to a different footing. Parliament represented a wider spectrum of the population than those whose interests had been protected by Magna Carta. It provided a more effective way of ventilating grievances against the king's government. Above all, it brought into existence a precocious system of national taxation, which did not depend on feudal obligation but on the consent of the Parliamentary Commons. Future constitutional struggles under Edward II and Richard II were not about feudal incidents. They were about mechanisms for making the king responsible to the wider community. Under Edward II, and again under Richard II and Henry VI, the great issue was control over the membership and powers of the royal council, which emerged in the late middle ages as the nerve centre of the king's government. These were things about which Magna Carta had nothing to say.

Gradually, the English forgot about Magna Carta. Citations of the charter in the Year Books become progressively more infrequent. Parliamentary petitions for the charter to be confirmed, which had once been routine, disappear after 1416. Sir John Fortescue, a former Chief Justice of King's Bench, wrote the first general account of the English constitution in the 1460s. But although he was a firm believer in limited monarchy and the rule of law, he derived it from

Aristotle and Aquinas, not from Magna Carta. Tudor England cared even less for Magna Carta. The period witnessed a considerable expansion of the king's prerogative power and the growing use of special conciliar courts such as Star Chamber, which declined to be bound by the common law. Much of this was politically controversial. But Magna Carta was rarely mentioned. Sir Thomas Smith, whose book, *The Commonwealth of England*, was written in the 1560s, does not mention it. It does not feature in Shakespeare's *King John*. On the rare occasions that it was invoked, it was usually in the context of disputes about the Crown's control over the Church. It is one of the ironies of the period that Catholic traditionalists of the 1530s and the Puritan opponents of the religious policies of Queen Elizabeth both appealed to the first article of Magna Carta, which protected the liberties of the Church, although the Church was by now a nationalised industry with the monarch as its non-executive chairman. 'Where is now become the Great Charter of England, obtained by so many difficulties?', asked the Puritan lawyer James Morice in the Parliament of 1593. It was a good question.

Magna Carta as we know it was reinvented in the early seventeenth century, largely by one man, the judge and politician Sir Edward Coke. A man of prodigious learning and bilious disposition, Coke rose to become Chief Justice of King's Bench. He fell out with King James I as a result of James's interference in the working of the courts. Coke objected to this, as a result of which he was dismissed in November 1616. For the remaining eighteen years of his life he was to be a determined opponent of the pretensions of the Stuart monarchy. Coke transformed Magna Carta from a somewhat technical catalogue of feudal regulations into the foundation document of the English constitution, a status that it has enjoyed ever since among the large community of commentators who have never actually read it. In their final form, Coke's views about Magna Carta were embodied in the second book of his *Institutes of the Laws of England*. In this remarkable treatise, Coke read almost the whole common law of England into the text of Magna Carta. He described Articles 39 and 40 as pure gold, every syllable of which was to be studied. He regarded it as the origin of the writ of habeas corpus and of trial by jury. More generally, Coke took the provisions of the charter that protected a man's 'liberties', which actually meant his privileges and immunities, and treated them as referring to the liberty of the subject. This meant, according to him, that all invasions of personal liberty by the Crown were unlawful. He even suggested that Magna Carta was the origin of parliamentary sovereignty, although no Parliament existed for half a century after it was sealed. He asserted that it prevented the exaction of money by the Crown without consent, although the only clauses dealing with taxation in the charter of 1215 had been removed in subsequent reissues. In short, said Coke in the parliamentary debates over the Petition of Right on 1628, Magna Carta was a charter for limited monarchy. 'Magna Carta', he famously declared, 'is such a fellow that he will have no sovereign.'

Many people who revere Magna Carta have never heard of Sir Edward Coke. Yet he has had an extraordinary influence over our perceptions of the charter. Coke's *Institutes* were regarded as a work of high authority until the nineteenth century. His analysis of Magna Carta was swallowed wholesale by the early American colonists. The framers of the US Constitution and the federal and state Bills of Rights deployed Magna Carta against the government of George III, just as Coke had deployed it against Charles I. The due process clause of the fifth and fourteenth Amendments, is based on Article 39 as interpreted by Coke. In 1991, it was calculated that Magna Carta had been cited in more than 900 decisions of state and federal courts to date, generally in support of propositions that would not have been recognised by the barons at Runnymede. It had been relied upon in more than sixty Supreme Court decisions in the previous half-century. 'The safeguards of due process of law and the equal protection of the laws,' wrote Justice Frankfurter in his judgment in *Malinki v New York* 324 US 401, 413 (1945), 'summarise the history of the freedom of English-speaking peoples running back to Magna Carta and reflected in the constitutional development of our people.' As recently as 2004, Justice Stephens, delivering the judgment of the majority of the US Supreme Court in *Rasul v Bush* 542 US 466 (2004), which allowed habeas corpus to prisoners in Guantanamo Bay, cited Article 39 of Magna Carta in support of his conclusion.

Ironically, Magna Carta has fared less well in the courts of the country in which it was born. Currently only three clauses of Magna Carta remain on the statute book. Even they have a certain archaic ring. They are the clause protecting the privileges of the Church, the clause protecting the privileges of the City of London, and the twenty-ninth clause of the 1225 charter, which reproduces Articles 39 and 40 of the 1215 document. I have quoted the essence of it above. Magna Carta has been cited in nearly 170 judgments of the superior courts in England since 1900. In almost every case, the reference has been to Article 29 of the 1225 Charter. In almost every case, it has been largely rhetorical. On the rare occasions when the courts have been presented with a case in which it might actually make a difference, the judges have shied away. Quite recently, a case was decided in the Appellate Committee of the House of Lords in which it might have been decisive. The case was *R v Secretary of State for the Foreign and Commonwealth Office ex parte Bancoult* [2009] 1 AC 453. It arose out of the Crown's prerogative power to make laws for British colonies. It exercised this power in 1971 by making an ordinance expelling the entire population of the British island of Diego Garcia in the Indian Ocean so that it could become a US military base. Colonial laws were valid only so far as they were consistent with English law. So the issue was whether the ordinance was consistent with the twenty-ninth clause of the 1225 version of Magna Carta. The House of Lords held the ordinance to be valid. Lord Hoffmann, speaking for the majority of the committee, acknowledged that Magna Carta forbade exile unless authorised by law. But, he said, it did not curtail the power of the lawmaker to make whatever laws it saw fit. In his view the right that it created was not so fundamental that the Crown could not take it away in the exercise of its prerogative power to make law for the colonies. Sir Edward Coke would be turning in his grave. But Lord Hoffmann was right. Magna Carta guarantees very little.

Yet Magna Carta matters, if not for the reasons commonly put forward. Some documents are less important for what they actually say than for what people wrongly think that they say. Some legislation has a symbolic significance quite distinct from any principle which it actually enacts. Thus it is with Magna Carta. It has become part of the rhetoric of a libertarian tradition based on the rule of law that represents a precocious and distinctively English contribution to western political theory. But we have to stop thinking about it just as a medieval document. It is really a chapter in the constitutional history of seventeenth-century England and eighteenth-century America.

Ultimately, one's attitude to political myths of this kind depends on where one situates one's golden age. Those who created the myths that surround Magna Carta located their golden age in the past. Their ideal was the recapture of an imagined paradise lost. To Coke and his generation it really mattered that the common law as they understood it in the seventeenth century should have existed in much the same form since the days of Edward the Confessor, King Alfred or the legendary Brutus the Trojan. The authority of their legal programme depended in large measure on its supposed antiquity. Otherwise, they would have been mere revolutionaries and not the respectable English gentlemen that they believed themselves to be. Today, the pendulum has swung the other way. 'Medieval' has become a synonym for barbarous. We are frighteningly ignorant of the past, in large measure because we no longer look to it as a source of inspiration. We are all revolutionaries now, controlling our own fate. So when we commemorate Magna Carta, perhaps the first question that we should ask ourselves is this: do we really need the force of myth to sustain our belief in democracy? Do we need to derive our belief in democracy and the rule of law from a group of muscular conservative millionaires from the north of England, who thought in French, knew no Latin or English, and died more than three quarters of a millennium ago? I rather hope not.

This essay was originally an address to the Friends of the British Museum in 2015 to mark the opening of the Museum's exhibition on Magna Carta and the 800th anniversary of the Charter, an occasion for a great outpouring of platitudinous humbug and national self-congratulation.

4

ARCANA IMPERII: STATE SECRETS
THROUGH THE AGES

For most of recorded history, governments have guarded their inner workings from the prying eyes of potentially hostile outsiders. The *'arcana imperii'* of my title was a phrase coined 2,000 years ago by the Roman historian Tacitus in the section of his history that deals with the year AD 69, the 'year of the four emperors'. He used it to describe the process by which men obtained and kept political power, a process in which he believed that secrecy played an essential role. The idea that concealment might also be essential to the effective exercise of power is more recent. It dates from the origin of the modern impersonal state in the sixteenth century. Its earliest articulate exponent was the Florentine diplomat and publicist Niccolo Machiavelli, who asserted that concealment was the foundation of the power of the state both within its territory and outside. Machiavelli has not had a good press. But this particular view has been treated as self-evident by most governments at most times. In Britain, every new privy councillor to this day swears an oath, the language of which dates back to 1570, in which he swears to 'keep secret all matters committed and revealed unto you or that shall be treated of secretly in council'.

I am not going to recite a long list of things that governments have tried to keep secret over the centuries. I would like to consider a different question; namely does it matter? A century and a half ago, the Victorian sage and future Regius Professor of History at Cambridge, Lord Acton, expressed the view that there was a natural conflict between the interest of historians in recording the past and the interest of officials in maintaining the confidentiality of their records. There was, he said, a 'great enmity between the truth of history and reasons of state, between sincere quest and official secrecy'. Contemporary historians have generally been content to echo his views on this point. Early disclosure is essential to their craft. But I want to suggest that while there are some cases in which official secrecy is the enemy of historical research, in the longer term they are complementary.

Leaving aside the rather special case of information whose disclosure would be prejudicial to national security, there are two main reasons why the government might wish to prevent access to its administrative records. One is to protect the historical reputation of the state, by withholding disclosure of documents that might make people think ill of it. This is in reality a form of indirect censorship. It seeks to distort the truth. It may require the suppression of documents for very long periods of time. No self-respecting historian is likely to support it. The second reason is to protect the decision-making process itself. The object is to encourage the frank discussion of the issues among decision-makers and their advisers, which may be inhibited if the discussion is shortly to be made public. This is not an attempt to distort the historical record. On the contrary, it may be fundamental to the integrity of the historical record. Without secrecy the discussion may not occur at all, or it may occur in a less formal setting where it will not be properly recorded. This is an area in which the concerns of historians and officials largely coincide, because in the long term it is more important to the writing of history that a record should exist, and that it should be accurate and complete, than that it should be immediately available.

When Lord Acton condemned official secrecy, he was mainly concerned with secrecy imposed for overtly propagandist reasons. In his day, the most notable practitioner of this kind of censorship was his particular bugbear, the papacy. The Vatican Archive, one of the most impressive collections of administrative documents in Europe, containing documents going back more than a millennium, was completely closed to outside researchers until 1883. Indeed, secrecy was so fundamental to its traditions that an inscription carved over the main entrance to the archives from the Vatican library pronounced the automatic excommunication of any stranger to the papal service who might enter there. This is not, as some people think, an invention of Dan Brown's. The reason for the policy was that popes had for many years regarded the spiritual authority of the Catholic Church as intimately dependent on its historical claim to be the sole authentic voice of a Christian tradition extending back to St Peter. Such controversial episodes in the history of the papacy as the reign of the Borgia pope Alexander VI, the trials of Bruno and Galileo for heresy, and the inner history of the Council of Trent were thought to have the potential to undermine the Church's mission.

This kind of attitude was becoming rare in Acton's time. But it was by no means unique and is not extinct today. The will of Frederick the Great of Prussia, who died in 1786, was treated as a classified document in the Prussian national archives on the directions of the German Foreign Ministry until 1916. Large parts of the central archives of the Italian state, dealing with the unification of Italy and the administration of Count Cavour in the 1850s, remained closed until well after the First World War. Defending this policy in 1912, the Italian prime minister Giolitti observed with disarming frankness that 'it would not be right to allow our beautiful legends to be undermined by mere historical criticism'. More recently, access to files covering the Second World War at the central archive of the Russian Ministry of Defence at Podolsk outside Moscow has been severely curtailed in order to protect the official narrative. In Turkey, it is reported that the central state archive, which is part of the secretariat of the prime minister, makes available files on sensitive subjects, such as the Ottoman Empire's dealings with the Armenians, on a highly selective basis.

It would be satisfying to record that considerations of this kind had never been an issue in Britain. But it would be untrue. The public records have always offered opportunities for political point-scoring to which British governments have occasionally been quite as sensitive as nineteenth-century popes. The scientific study of archives as a historical source begins in the seventeenth century. In England it was attended by political controversy from the outset. Chief Justice Sir Edward Coke gave it as his opinion, in the Fourth Part of his *Institutes*, that 'letters and writing concerning matters of state are not fit to be made vulgar'. In fact, the records of the main departments of state were so insecurely held in his time that it was in practice quite easy to get access to them. The parliamentary opposition to the first two Stuart kings included a number of competent antiquaries and historians, such as John Selden, Sir Robert Cotton and Sir Symonds d'Ewes, who saw in the public records a stick with which to beat the king. They scoured the records of the Middle Ages for material to support their case about the autonomy and privileges of Parliament. They went through the accounts of the medieval Exchequer in order to demonstrate that unlike Charles I, earlier kings had been able to fund their governments without resort to taxation. They produced examples of the English kings' defence of England's national interest to compare with what they saw as the craven conduct of con-temporary ministers. Charles I's decision in 1629 to seize the library of Sir Robert Cotton, which included a large number of originals and transcripts derived from the public records, shows that some of these attacks hit home.

The English civil war was followed by a period of rela-tive openness, at any rate for those researchers who were willing to confront the problems of physical dispersal, rats, damp, and the almost complete absence of inventories. At the beginning of the eighteenth century, England became the first country in Europe to publish a large part of its diplomatic archives. The twenty folio volumes of Rymer's *Foedera* were originally commissioned by William III's first minister, Lord Halifax. Rymer was the royal librarian. He published in full many thousands of diplomatic instructions and memoranda, account books, administrative instructions and treaties relating to English foreign policy between 1100 and 1654. This was something that no European government had ever done before, or indeed since, until well into the nineteenth century. The *Foedera* is still, to this day, the basic tool of research into the foreign relations of England's medi-eval kings.

It is ironic that in Britain the main occasion for the revival of censorship of the archives was the creation in the mid nineteenth century of the Public Record Office. This event made it necessary for the first time to devise rules govern-ing what could be made available to researchers, and what could not. For many years, each department was left to make its own rules. They were often overtly designed to protect the image of the state against criticism. When the Public Record Office first opened its doors to readers in 1856, the Foreign Office insisted that nothing later than 1628 could be disclosed. Among the documents restricted in this way were a large number that had actually been published by Rymer.

In the following year, the closure date was changed to 1760, where it remained until after the First World War. When in 1891 the master of the rolls, who was then responsible for the Public Record Office, had the date moved forward to 1830, the Foreign Office had the decision reversed. There was, they said, 'no sufficient guarantee against the admission of undesirable persons' [i.e. foreigners] to the reading rooms. As a result, the records of English foreign policy after 1760 could be consulted only with the permission of the secretary of state, and then only on terms that the researcher submitted his notes to the Foreign Office for review. They were frequently returned with extensive sections blocked out in ink. The main result of this policy, as the Oxford historian H. A. L. Fisher pointed out, was that British foreign policy in the century after 1760 was generally studied through the eyes of Britain's historic rivals, notably France and Germany, whose diplomatic archives for this period were for the most part open.

At the beginning of the twentieth century, even the domestic archives of the period of the revolutionary and Napoleonic wars were regarded as too sensitive for disclosure. The prime minister, Arthur Balfour, intervened personally in 1902 to veto a proposal to open all documents up to 1815, on the ground that even after the passage of a century the disclosure of documents relating to the government of Ireland was 'full of contentious matter which bears on slumbering, though not yet deceased controversies'. Others objected that the opening of the archives of this period would undermine relations with France by revealing the scale on which Britain had funded the domestic opposition to its rulers during the revolutionary and Napoleonic wars. There is something rather touching about the confidence of these public servants that British undercover operations of an earlier age were still secret in 1902. In fact, much the best source of information about them is the files of the French chief of police Joseph Fouché. They had been open to readers in the French national archives for some time, and some of them were already in the process of being published by Alphonse Aulard and other French scholars.

It was not until the interwar years that the rules were relaxed so as to make possible the serious study of modern English history, even by 'undesirable persons'. However, the real landmark in this area was the Public Records Act of 1958. The Act reflected the recommendations of the Grigg Committee, which had reported in 1954. It removed the right of individual departments to make their own rules and introduced a standard closed period of fifty years, except in the case of documents the disclosure of which would be damaging to national security or which contained confidential information about individuals still living. Exceptions were to be considered by the Lord Chancellor's Advisory Council on the Public Records, a statutory body comprising officials, historians, archivists and other experts, whose assessments were objective, well-informed and almost invariably followed. The fifty-year period was overtly designed to protect the decision-making process, not the historic reputation of the state. It had been proposed by the Grigg Committee because it was thought to represent the maximum duration of a political career. Of course, like any closed period, the fifty-year rule was liable to suppress politically embarrassing information as well. But that was not the object of the exercise nor, of course, its effect in the long term. There has, since 1958, been very little scope for discretionary decisions designed to mould the conclusions of historians or restrict the use that unfriendly persons might make of the public records.

More recently, the whole concept of protecting the decision-making process has been challenged. The closure period was reduced to thirty years in 1968. It has been progressively reduced since. The Thirty Year Rule Review Panel, which reported on the question in 2009, recommended fifteen years, and some of the witnesses who gave evidence before it would have preferred a period as short as five. The current practice is to keep documents closed for ten years except for certain categories of personal information, where the period may be longer. These changes raise far more difficult questions than the kind of censorship that used to be the main preoccupation of government departments.

The first point to be made is that reading an official document in the National Archives is no longer the main way in which its contents may see the light of day. It is probably less significant than the two main avenues of unofficial disclosure, namely the memoirs of ex-ministers and civil servants; and the growth of a culture of leaking, fed in part by hostility to the whole notion of secrecy in the public service, and in part by a rejection of hierarchy, which leads individuals to feel that they should follow their own consciences in deciding what the public ought to know. These things represent a major change in our political culture. During the Second World War, about 12,000 men and women served at one time or another at the Government Code and Cypher School at Bletchley Park, most of them young and recently recruited from the ordinary peacetime occupations to which they returned in 1945. Several hundred more were cleared to receive the intelligence that Bletchley Park generated. There was no value in keeping the work of Bletchley Park secret for as long as it was. Yet the culture of public affairs at the time meant that not one of the many individuals involved disclosed the existence of wartime Ultra until 1974, when the officer responsible for controlling the distribution of Ultra before 1945 published his memoirs. This is a generational thing. That degree of reticence would be inconceivable today.

I have no position on the question of whether the current belief in disclosure is good or bad for our standards of government and public administration. I doubt whether a single answer to that question is even possible. But I think that we need to be more honest with ourselves about the impact that it will have on the quality of the sources that will be available to future historians writing about the events of our own day. Of course, plenty will be written. But how reliable will it be?

I specialise in a period of history, namely the late middle ages, when no one had any reason to ask this question. Although the use of documentary evidence for the writing of history was not unknown in the middle ages (official documents are quite often quoted in chronicles), the idea of opening the archives of the state to outsiders for the purpose of research was unheard of. There are, however, some basic points about the nature of historical evidence that are broadly true in all periods. As a general rule, the more self-conscious a historical record is, the less valuable it is as a source of information. Take a royal proclamation of the kind issued by the Tudors to communicate with their subjects en masse. It was intended to be read out at the sound of a bell in market squares across the country. It is a highly self-conscious source, deliberately contrived to make an impact on the public, perhaps as much by what it suppressed as by what it declared. As evidence of the government's thinking, its value is limited by its public character and rhetorical purpose. The confidential memorandum that proposed it, or the record of the Privy Council at which it was discussed, are likely to tell us much more. The same point may be made by reference to the archives of diplomatic exchange. The English diplomat Sir Henry Wootton, who represented Elizabeth I and James I over many years at the courts of Germany and Italy, memorably defined an ambassador as an 'honourable man sent forth to lie for his country abroad'. The ambassador's formal instruction, which was a public document delivered to the court to which he was accredited as evidence of his authority, was a self-conscious statement, and as such almost useless as a historical source. The private instructions of a medieval or Renaissance diplomat, which told him what he was expected to achieve and how, is likely to be far more valuable to the historian. The deliberations of the council that prepared it will probably be more valuable still. Quite often, the best source for some fact is a document that incidentally records it in the course of fulfilling some utterly humdrum function: for example, an entry in the Exchequer accounts recording a payment to a diplomatic messenger, to a spy for an undercover mission or to a soldier for some unheroic enterprise. The reason for this is that of all government records, accounting documents are probably the least self-conscious. The clerk who writes them is likely to have little interest in the subject matter and none at all in the impact that it may make on outsiders or later historians.

I make these points in order to suggest that the prospect of publicity is a major source of bias in governmental documents. The problem about prematurely disclosing them is that the knowledge that this will happen adds a significant and unwelcome element of self-consciousness to their contents. It leads to selective and sometimes tendentious omissions. It encourages a level of generality that omits historically important but politically equivocal detail. It often causes the document to be written in a way that means much less to outsiders than to those who made it. All of this tends to undermine the integrity of the historical record.

The Radcliffe Committee, reporting in 1976 on the principles that should govern the publication of ministerial memoirs, identified three categories of information that ministers should not be permitted to disclose. The first two categories comprise information the disclosure of which would contravene the requirements of national security or damage this country's relationship with other governments. The third category, which is the one germane to my present theme, is both more controversial and more difficult to define. This comprises information the disclosure of which would be destructive of confidential relationships within government. Justifying this category in their report, Lord Radcliffe's committee observed:

> ... the argument in its favour is quite simple and does not gain by elaboration ... Those who are to act together in pursuance of a policy agreed in common do require and expect the observance of confidence as to what they say to each other; and unless they can be assured of the maintenance of that confidence they will not speak easily or frankly among themselves. Opinions, perhaps unpopular, perhaps embarrassing, will be muted or suppressed if they are known to be liable to future disclosure at the whim of some retired colleague. Business which should be discussed by the whole body will tend to be settled by two or three in a corner.

The principle that candour in the expressing and recording of opinions depends on confidentiality was already well established when Radcliffe reported in 1976. But it had never been easy to enforce. During the nineteenth century, English governments had few tools at their disposal for enforcing the confidentiality of the decision-making process, other than persuasion and social pressure. This sometimes worked. More often it did not. After the death of the prime minister, George Canning, in 1827, ministers went to considerable lengths, with very little success, to prevent his widow from commissioning a biography based on his personal papers.

They were concerned that it would expose the bitter arguments over Catholic emancipation that had divided recent administrations. Half a century later, the posthumous publication of the diaries of Charles Greville, in which the diarist had patiently recorded the inner debates and scandals of the political class over the forty years that he had served as clerk to the Privy Council, was regarded as a profoundly shocking event. Queen Victoria denounced the author's 'indiscretion, indelicacy, ingratitude, betrayal of confidence, and shameful disloyalty towards his sovereign'. Obscure pressures on Greville's literary executor and publisher resulted in substantial parts of the diary being cut out of the published version, and when the manuscript was presented to the British Museum in 1895, the trustees directed that it should not be made available to readers. It was not published in full until the 1930s.

These challenges to the conventional secrecy of government were, however, rare until after the First World War, when a flood of memoir-writers, diarists and manipulative leakers provoked the first systematic attempts to enforce the confidentiality of the decision-making process. The advent of a Labour government in 1929, which was both bitterly divided and relatively inexperienced, brought many of these issues to a head. After the controversial decision of the Cabinet in August 1931 to reduce unemployment benefit by 10 per cent, the *Daily Herald* published on 24 August a complete and accurate account of the discussion, with the names of the ministers who had voted against. This disclosure exposed the divisions of the government and made it impossible for ministers to maintain a united front against the critics in their own party. The leak, which was intended to force the government back on to the path of ideological rectitude, in fact had exactly the opposite effect. The government resigned that afternoon. The conservative-dominated National Government endorsed the reductions. Whether the

Daily Herald's disclosure was constitutionally desirable is a difficult question. The fact that the general election that followed returned the National Government with the largest parliamentary majority ever enjoyed by a British government may suggest that it served the cause of democratic choice. However, for a historian, what matters is that the discussion of expenditure cuts around the Cabinet table would certainly not have been as open as it was if the leak had been anticipated. The decision would have been fixed in advance of the Cabinet meeting in the course of private discussions between much smaller groups of ministers. We would know a great deal less about it today.

That at any rate seems to have been the view of the Cabinet Secretary, Sir Maurice Hankey. After 1931 he inaugurated a number of rules about the retention of papers by ministers, access to sensitive policy documents by non-official persons, and prosecutions in the case of the more egregious breaches. When, in 1934, Edgar Lansbury, the son of the then leader of the Labour Party, published a book about his father's career which quoted extensively from Cabinet papers of the former Labour government, he was charged under the Official Secrets Act and fined. Official papers were energetically retrieved by the Cabinet Office from serving and former ministers. Some, including Churchill and Lloyd George, were grand enough to resist. Most were not. When the former prime minister Arthur Balfour died in 1930, he left his private papers to his niece Blanche Dugdale to enable her to write the official biography. She subsequently gave them to the library of the British Museum. But the Cabinet Office prevailed upon the trustees of the museum to close them, as a result of which they were not available to readers until 1968.

It is doubtful whether either the Cabinet Office or the trustees of the museum had any legal right to act as they did. Nevertheless, Hankey's principles survived more or less intact until the 1970s, when they began to break down under pressures very similar to those that had destroyed the previous, informal system before 1931. The publication of the first volume of *The Crossman Diaries* in 1975 was a landmark in this process. The Labour government of 1964–70 contained an unusually large number of diarists. However, Crossman was special because he deliberately set out to challenge the conventions concerning the secrecy surrounding government decision-making, of which he disapproved. On 26 January 1967 there was a discussion in Cabinet about ministerial diaries, following a report in the *Observer* that Richard Crossman and Barbara Castle were both writing one. The discussion is recorded in different terms in the official minute in the Public Record Office and in the diaries of several of the participants. The problem discussed was not of course the mere keeping of diaries, but the possibility of premature publication. Both Crossman and Castle were reported to have signed contracts with publishers. George Brown, then foreign secretary, was concerned about the implications for the openness of discussion in Cabinet and appears to have had substantial support from other ministers. Harold Wilson spoke from a lengthy brief prepared by the Cabinet Office to the same effect. Tony Benn said that he too was a diarist, and what he objected to was that he had not been approached by a publisher with a contract. However, what mainly exercised the ministers around the table was the possibility that Crossman's diary might be published before the next election. Some pointed out that even if publication was delayed until after the next election, if there was a very narrow Labour or Tory majority, followed by another election, and Crossman's diaries came out between the two, it would do enormous damage to the fortunes of the Labour Party.

This incident, like the affair of *Daily Herald* in 1931, suggests a more general conclusion about the place of Cabinet secrecy in our current constitution. The original purpose of Cabinet secrecy in the eighteenth and early nineteenth centuries was to support the doctrine of collective ministerial responsibility. Secrecy enabled ministers and their advisers to discuss their differences freely without exposing them to the king, who might otherwise be enabled to pick off some of them against the others. Instead, he was faced with his ministers' conclusions apparently endorsed by them *en bloc*. Clearly, the need to limit monarchical discretion is no longer a relevant factor. But that does not mean that the collective responsibility of ministers is redundant. Its modern function is to enable a government to discuss its differences internally while maintaining a common front in the face of its own party and the electorate. Whether or not we regard this as a good thing, it seems to me that for as long as parties remain the basis of our political system it is an inevitable thing. The only consequence of candour in ministerial memoirs or diaries will be that the same discussions will occur elsewhere, out of the hearing of the diarists or minute-takers. Richard Crossman was able to assure his colleagues that the terms of his contract with his publishers would ensure that the diaries were not published until well after an election. If he had told them that extracts might appear at any moment or just before an election campaign, it seems clear that Cabinet discussions in his presence would have been limited to matters that were unlikely to be controversial or to expose divisions in the party, while the real discussion would have occurred in small cabals elsewhere.

The publication of *The Crossman Diaries* gave rise to the only court decision on this issue. Lord Widgery, then the Lord Chief Justice, accepted the principle of the collective responsibility of ministers and the confidentiality of governmental decision-making. But his judgment is mainly important for establishing that the confidential character of governmental decision-making was not absolutely enforceable, but only conditional on the court's assessment of the public interest. The critical factor in Lord Widgery's view was that the first volume of Crossman's diaries would appear ten years after the events it covered. That, in his view, was long enough to serve the relevant public interest. He therefore refused to grant an injunction against its publication. Today, it is unlikely that the courts would even require ten years to have passed, unless the subject matter fell within one of the first two of the Radcliffe categories, relating to national security or foreign relations, and perhaps not always then.

In practice, in the last twenty years Lord Radcliffe's third category (documents tending to undermine relations of confidence within government) has been disregarded not just by the authors of ministerial and civil service memoirs but also by the Cabinet Office and the Foreign Office charged with enforcing it. The memoirs of ministers like Nigel Lawson, Lord Owen and Clare Short, and officials like Sir Christopher Meyer and Dame Stella Rimington, are cases in point. The reluctance of the Cabinet Office to insist on the third of the Radcliffe principles is understandable. The decisions of the courts are at best equivocal. Moreover, injunction or no injunction, the confidential character of a text, once it has been written, is difficult to maintain in the age of international publishing and the internet. Lance Price's 2005 memoirs of life in No. 10 were substantially altered at the request of the Cabinet Secretary. But the *Daily Mail*, to whom Price had sold the serialisation rights, subsequently obtained, without his authority, a copy of the unexpurgated version and published extracts side by side with the final text.

There is a case, which has been made by Sir Christopher Meyer and Clare Short, for example, that cultural changes have killed off confidential relationships within government anyway. There is also a case, which was made by Richard

Crossman, that even if these relationships subsist, they are less important than satisfying the legitimate interest of the public in knowing how government works. There is something in both of these points, although perhaps not as much as their authors believe. However, I believe that both points are misguided for a different reason, namely that they are self-defeating. They underestimate the desire of officials and ministers to be able to discuss issues confidentially. The likelihood is that they will take avoiding action so that they can continue to do so. In a revealing passage from his evidence to the Thirty Year Review Panel, Lord Wakeham remarked that when he was in government, between 1979 and 1994, he told his officials that they were never to put before him for his signature a letter that would be embarrassing if it appeared on the front page of the next day's *Guardian*. Now there are, of course, two possible interpretations of this interesting instruction. One, which I do not for a moment believe, is that Lord Wakeham never intended, in his capacity as a minister of the Crown, to say anything that would be unpleasing to readers of the *Guardian*. The other is that whenever he had something to say that readers of the *Guardian* would not like, he would make sure that it was not recorded in writing.

The decline in the standard of government record-keeping over the past twenty-five years or so is a phenomenon which has often been noticed by those who are well placed to judge. In recent years it has been associated with a tendency for critical decisions to be made by very small and informally constituted groups of ministers; what has been called 'sofa government'. The tendency emerges very clearly from, for example, the 2004 report of the Butler Committee on the use of intelligence on weapons of mass destruction. I do not want to suggest that the fear of leaks or premature disclosure is the only factor at work here. But it seems obvious that it is a significant factor, and that the recording of government decision-making is the poorer for it. When writing this essay I consulted a number of recently retired senior civil servants about their practices. The sample is statistically insignificant; seven. It has also been assembled on a wholly unscientific basis, namely that they were all people whom I happened to know well enough to ask the question and expect an honest answer. With one exception, every one of them admitted to having omitted significant information from internal documents, which in earlier times they would have included, and to having communicated it informally instead so that they would not be recorded in writing. One of them remarked that in some departments it was common for politically sensitive matters to be omitted from documentary records and recorded only on marginal notes written on Post-It Notes. These would be removed and binned after the right people had seen them.

It is, of course, a great deal easier to identify these problems than to suggest ways of dealing with them. But I am bound to say that I regard the shortening of the closed period for public documents as unfortunate. The Thirty Year Review Panel accepted the third of the Radcliffe categories in principle. They also appear to have accepted the basic rationale of the thirty-year rule, namely that documents recording the making of government policy should not be disclosed while those involved were liable to be still in government. But they considered that the period of closure should be reduced for two main reasons. One was that the Freedom of Information Act would result in the disclosure of much of the material anyway, without any delay at all. The other was that ministerial careers were getting shorter. The Freedom of Information Act is in my view a red herring. It is subject to extensive exceptions, which include all three of Lord Radcliffe's categories of sensitive information. In particular, Section 35 exempts information relating to the formulation or development of government policy and ministerial communications, including proceedings of the Cabinet. As for the suggestion that ministerial careers were getting shorter, that was based on a sample heavily weighted by recent and rather untypical experience. The long period of Tory government between 1979 and 1997, and the almost as long period of Labour government between 1997 and 2010, have each had the effect of clearing out the old guard in the opposing party. The result was that when the opposing party finally came to power, its leaders rarely had any record in government and were not likely to be embarrassed by the disclosure of the earlier contributions to discussions within government. But we cannot assume that long periods of single party government are going to be the rule in future. We need not resort to extreme examples, such as Winston Churchill, whose ministerial career spanned forty-seven years. In 2014, Kenneth Clarke was sitting in Cabinet as Minister without Portfolio. He had first attended Cabinet in 1972, forty-two years before. In the same government the foreign secretary, William Hague, first became a minister twenty-four years before, and had sat in his first Cabinet nineteen years before. The period of time during which civil servants can expect to influence policy has certainly not reduced. Indeed, it can be expected to increase now that it has become easier to serve beyond the traditional retiring age of sixty. Of course none of this addresses the problem of leaks or ministerial memoirs. There is not much that can be done about leaks other than to pay more attention to the dissemination of information within the public service. As for ministerial and civil service memoirs, it seems to me that public servants should not be at liberty to decide for themselves to disclose information that they have acquired in their capacity as servants of the state and which the state withholds for considered reasons of public policy.

Underlying all of these considerations is a basic fact of human nature which it is unrealistic to ignore. As Thomas Carlyle observed in his *History of Frederick the Great*, 'men are very porous, weighty secrets oozing out of them like quicksilver though clay jars'. The natural sensitivity of public figures to the impact of their discussions on outsiders will inevitably influence what they will allow to appear in official documents if these are liable to be released in the course of their careers. Perhaps the last word on this question can be left to Harold Wilson. During the debate in Cabinet on *The Crossman Diaries*, to which I have already referred, he said that he proposed to write his own memoirs three times. There would be a sober factual account, drawing on information in the public domain, which he would publish as soon as he left office. A second, somewhat more candid account, would appear after he finally retired from politics. And a final version containing the real truth would be left with his papers to be published after his death. I ask you, which one would you rather read?

This was originally a lecture delivered in memory of an old friend, Adrian Cooper, in June 2018. An earlier, and different version, had previously been delivered to the Friends of the National Archives in June 2010. I have updated it to take account of recent changes.

5

THE DISUNITED KINGDOM:
ENGLAND, IRELAND AND SCOTLAND

Article 1 of the Act of Union of 1707 provides that 'the two kingdoms of Scotland and England shall on the 1st of May and for ever after be united into one kingdom by the name of Great Britain'. These words marked the birth, three centuries ago, of Great Britain. The United Kingdom had longer to wait. In 1800, nearly a century after the Act of Union with Scotland, Article 1 of the Act of Union with Ireland provided that the kingdom should henceforth be known as the United Kingdom of Great Britain and Ireland. Uniquely among the nation states of Europe, the British state was founded on two legislative unions: one between England and Scotland, which has lasted more than three centuries and was until recently remarkably successful; the other between England and Ireland, which was a tragic failure from the outset and broke up in less than half that time. It takes more than statutes to make a nation and more than statutes to unmake one. The history of Irish nationalism was already a long one when the union with Ireland broke up in 1922. It dated back certainly to the sixteenth century and was arguably older than that. By comparison, Scottish nationalism has a much shorter history. As a serious political movement, it dates only from the 1960s. Yet it narrowly failed to win a referendum on independence in 2014 and commands a majority of the Scottish Parliament created in 1999.

The rise of powerful internal nationalisms within the territory of ancient states is a worldwide phenomenon, which raises some fundamental questions about the identity of nations. Most states are composites, built out of territories that were once autonomous. Often, the component parts conserve their own distinctive ethnic, religious, cultural or political traditions. Britain, Spain, Belgium, Italy and Germany are notable European examples. Some of these composite states have recently begun to fracture. Five centuries after the union of the component kingdoms of Spain, separatist parties have a majority in the Catalan regional legislature and in 2017 tried to secede unilaterally. Belgium, which in spite of its artificial origins and linguistic diversity, has enjoyed a formidable cohesion for most of its history, is threatened with break-up by renascent linguistic nationalist parties. In Italy there has been serious talk, although as yet no more than that, about the industrial north seceding from the state created 150 years ago by Garibaldi and Cavour. But perhaps the most remarkable example lies further east. Kiev was the first nucleus of the Russian nation, but after ten centuries in which the fortunes of Russia and Ukraine seemed indissolubly linked, it is now the capital of an independent state. It is clear that there is nothing predestined or immutable about the identity of nations.

In 1882, the French historian Ernest Renan delivered a famous lecture at the Sorbonne entitled 'What is a nation?'. Writing at a time when national sentiment in Europe had never been stronger, Renan questioned all of the theories of national identity current in his own day, most of which were based on ethnic and linguistic solidarities. In his view, the identity of a nation depended entirely on collective sentiment. It was therefore inherently changeable. Nations, he said, depended for their continued existence on a 'daily referendum' among its population. If once they ceased to feel like a nation, they would cease to be one. So far as existing national identities had any stability, this was due to the accumulated weight of historic myth. A nation, Renan wrote, was the culmination of a long history of collective effort, collective sacrifice and collective devotion. It depended on a consciousness of having done great things together in the past, and wanting to do more of them in future. The definition is pithier in French: *'avoir fait de grandes choses ensemble, vouloir en faire encore.'* What were these great things in a nation's past that fixed its identity? The examples that Renan gave – heroism, glory, great men – were those that would probably have occurred to most nineteenth-century thinkers. They were synonymous with war and conquest. Paraphrasing Renan, the Harvard political scientist Karl Deutsch observed, in language that has often been misattributed to Renan himself, that a nation is 'a group of people united by a mistaken view of their past and a common hatred of their neighbours'. Renan thought that the major European nation states of his own day would survive for centuries. Yet by his test even they were fragile constructs. Sentiments change. External threats recede to expose the fault lines within historic nations. The memory of joint triumphs fades away, to be replaced by the more durable recollection of real or imagined oppression and antagonism.

England is and always has been the dominant member of the United Kingdom. This is the inevitable consequence of its greater size and population, its powerful public institutions and its central geographical position. The formation and survival of the United Kingdom is therefore essentially the story of England's relations with the other nations of the British Isles. Historically, three factors have been dominant: religious allegiance, defence against external enemies and access to markets. What is missing from this catalogue is idealism. The unemotional origins of the United Kingdom differentiate it from European states like Italy and Germany that coalesced in a wave of patriotic emotion. Distinctive too has been the absence of any deliberate policy of assimilation by the British state, such as that which was energetically practised by the governments of post-revolutionary France and post-Risorgimento Italy. The British state has never consciously tried to mould a British nation. So far as a broader British identity emerged, it did so only spontaneously and after the unions, not before. In Ireland it never happened. In Scotland it did. The reasons for this divergence can tell us a lot about ourselves.

It is necessary to start with Ireland, whose shadow looms large over this issue. The partial separation of Ireland from the United Kingdom in 1922 marked Britain's greatest failure in the whole of its long history. It was also a conspicuous symptom of our lack of interest in creating a single nation out of the disparate but interdependent peoples of the British Isles. In 1800, at the time of the Irish Act of Union, Ireland represented about a quarter of the population of the United Kingdom, a far higher proportion than Scotland. For six centuries, Ireland had been a lordship belonging to the kings of England, but constitutionally separate from England. It had its own legislature, with separate houses of lords and commons, its own judiciary and its own executive. All of these institutions were miniatures of the equivalent institutions in England. For customs purposes, Ireland was another country separated by steep tariff barriers from its natural markets in England. Historically, Ireland's relationship with England had been essentially colonial. It was partly colonised from England in the twelfth century and again in the seventeenth. The twelfth-century colonisation was a superficial and ephemeral affair. The Anglo-Norman colonists were a numerically very small group whose economic and military dependence on alliances with the Irish chiefs meant that they were largely assimilated by the indigenous Irish by the end of the middle ages. It is a common fate of conquerors to be absorbed by those that they conquer, unless there is a wholesale displacement of population. The seventeenth-century colonisation was a far more thorough and brutal business, which not only did displace a large part of the population but also introduced into Ireland the corrosive religious divisions which plagued its relations with England until quite recently.

The Protestant religion, initially a minority creed, was imposed on the great majority of the population of England during the second half of the sixteenth century. This was possible in England because it was a highly centralised, intensively governed country, with an educated and influential elite that was already largely converted to one or other of the variant forms of Protestantism. None of these conditions obtained in Ireland. Protestantism made virtually no headway there. The continued Catholic allegiance of the mass of the Irish population was a serious problem for England at a time when her main external enemies, Spain in the sixteenth century and France in the seventeenth, were the leading Catholic powers of their time. Even in the eighteenth century, when the foreign policy of the great continental powers lost its confessional colours, the existence of a predominantly Catholic population in Ireland was seen as a major strategic weakness, by both England and its European enemies. As late as 1796, the French general Hoche, accompanied by the Irish nationalist Wolfe Tone, very nearly succeeded in landing an army of 15,000 men at Bantry Bay. Sir Roger Casement tried to do something similar with German support in 1916. It was the abiding fear that Ireland would become a backdoor into England for her continental enemies that had prompted the succession of brutal attempts at large-scale Protestant colonisation in the seventeenth century. It came in three main waves. At the beginning of the seventeenth century, the colonisation of the northern province of Ulster involved a massive displacement of the population in a very short period of time, transforming what had hitherto been the most intensely Gaelic region of Ireland into a largely Scottish and Presbyterian community. The reoccupation of Ireland by Oliver Cromwell in the 1650s, which marked the second wave, was even more brutal and geographically more extensive. It may have displaced or killed as much as a third of the indigenous population. The third wave was the invasion of the country by William of Orange at the end of the seventeenth century in order to forestall the threat from the deposed Stuart, King James II, and his ally Louis XIV of France. The Williamite invasion was not particularly bloody. But it was the most damaging of all for England's future relation with Ireland, for it was followed by a series of draconian statutes against the Catholic majority, which prevented them from holding land or offices, from bearing arms, from observing their religion, from holding schools, in fact from participating in almost every aspect of civil society. Few of these disabilities were applied to Catholics in England itself. Eighteenth-century English Catholics could not vote in parliamentary elections or sit in Parliament or hold offices of state or marry into the royal family. But they could do almost everything else, including own land and practise their religion. In the eighteenth century, the systematic persecution of Catholics was confined to the one part of the British Isles where they constituted the overwhelming majority of the population. The result was to create a caste-based system in Ireland, in which a Protestant minority of mainly English origin held a monopoly of political office and all of the land. As William Pitt the Younger told the House of Commons in 1799, all the problems of Ireland were ultimately due to 'the hereditary feud between two nations on the same land'.

At the time Pitt was speaking, the crunch moment for

this unsustainable system had arrived. The French Revolution had an immense impact in Ireland, not only among Catholics but among radicalised Irish Protestants who saw in the unequal relationship with England the roots of Ireland's political and economic backwardness. The United Irishmen, founded by the Protestant Wolfe Tone and others in 1791, adopted an overtly republican policy, and after the outbreak of the revolutionary war in the following year, they made alliance with revolutionary France the cornerstone of their policy. The Parliament in Dublin responded by embarking on a panic-stricken programme of concession and reform. Almost all of the statutory disabilities inflicted on Catholics since the end of the seventeenth century were repealed, apart from their exclusion from the Dublin Parliament itself. These rapid measures of liberalisation failed to draw the poison for two main reasons. The first was that it was too late. The French Revolution had unleashed passions which could not easily be contained. The progressive expansion of the franchise from 1832 onward broke the political power of land, marginalised the Protestant elite everywhere in Ireland except Ulster, and made it possible to organise a Home Rule movement on a national scale. The second reason was that the long-term consequences of the disabilities inflicted on Catholics for more than a century proved to be more difficult to address than the disabilities themselves. The most serious of these was the land problem. As a result of the systematic exclusion of Catholics from the ownership of real property throughout the eighteenth century, by 1800 substantially all the land in Ireland was in the hands of a minority defined first by its religious allegiance, and second, by its political dependence on England. In a pastoral and agricultural society, where land was the main source of social status and the only source of capital, this was a disaster. It might perhaps have been addressed by a wholesale redistribution of land of the kind that has actually happened in Ireland since 1922. There was never the slightest chance of this happening in Victorian Britain, with its profound attachment to the minimal state and to rights of property as the twin foundations of constitutional liberty.

In May 1798, there was a serious uprising in Ireland, accompanied by three attempts by French squadrons to land troops on the Irish coast. The rising was poorly organised and quickly suppressed. But 1798 left a poisonous legacy. Although the leaders of the rising declared their desire to unite Irishmen of both religions against English rule, in parts of the south the revolt was accompanied by bloody massacres of Protestants which transformed attitudes on both sides of the Irish Channel. Before 1798, an important minority of the Protestant community had supported Irish nationalism. United Irishmen, the leading independence movement, had originally been founded by Protestants in Belfast and their main strength lay in the Presbyterian north. The sectarian violence against Protestants put an end to the tradition of Protestant nationalism in Ireland. Almost overnight, it transformed Irish Protestants, then about a quarter of the population and the dominant element in the towns, into an embattled, pro-British minority. As the Irish historian William Lecky observed a generation later, the rising of 1798 planted in Ireland the seeds of sectarian hatred that remained thereafter 'the chief obstacle to all rational self-government'. In England, the prime minister, William Pitt the Younger, drew the same conclusion. In his view, peace in Ireland was indispensable if Britain was to prevail in the struggle with Napoleonic France. The maintenance of a Protestant Parliament in Dublin was no longer sustainable in a mainly Catholic country. Yet the admission of Catholics to the Irish Parliament would only serve to swamp the Protestant minority and perpetuate sectarian divisions. The solution adopted was to dilute the political passions dividing Ireland by abolishing its independent Parliament and incorporating Ireland into the larger political community of England.

In 1835, the great French political scientist Alexis de Tocqueville spent several weeks in Ireland speaking to Catholic and Protestant, from town and country alike. His notes, which he perhaps intended to write up into a book, are among the most revealing portraits of Ireland in the generation after the Act of Union. The most striking thing is the almost complete absence of bitterness or hatred among the educated. De Tocqueville was impressed by the genuine desire of the Protestant minority to improve the condition of all the people of Ireland. Yet, the overwhelming impression that he took away from his conversations with them was one of hopeless resignation in the face of the insoluble problems bequeathed by two centuries of prejudice and folly. De Tocqueville was a liberal Frenchman, a nobleman and a Catholic. He was also a great admirer of England. But his conclusion was that the same tradition of liberal aristocratic government which in his view had made English strong and rich, also accounted for the irredeemable failure of everything that they did in Ireland.

Modern mythology has tended to concentrate on the potato famine of 1846, on the fate of Gladstone's Home Rule policy and on the Easter Rising in 1916. But the Union was doomed well before these events. It did not even bring England the military security that had been Pitt's great object in 1800. In a speech delivered in Glasgow in 1871, Isaac Butt, the first leader of the Parliamentary Home Rule movement, said: 'We were told that the Union would make an invasion of Ireland impossible, but would an enemy be any worse received in Ireland by many of the people now than in 1798?'. It was a good question. There were important pro-German movements among Irish nationalists in both world wars of the twentieth century. In the closing days of the Second World War, the Irish President Eamon De Valera famously sent a message of condolence to the German ambassador on the death of Hitler.

I have dwelled upon the unhappy experience of Ireland's union with England because it is in almost every respect the polar opposite of Scotland's experience. In an essay written in 1881, the great constitutional lawyer A. V. Dicey noted the divergent fortunes of the Scottish and Irish unions over the previous century. His explanation was very simple. 'The shortest summary of the whole matter,' he wrote, 'is that all the special causes which favoured the incorporation of Scotland with England, were conspicuously wanting in the attempt to unite Ireland with Great Britain.'

What were these differences? In the first place, Scotland has never been an English colony, even though Lowland Scotland, like England itself, was occupied by the Normans in the eleventh century, and recent migrants from England still account for more than a tenth of Scotland's population. Except for a very short period in the late thirteenth and early fourteenth centuries, there has never been a sustained English occupation of Scotland. Second, Scotland had never been a subordinate lordship. Before the union it was an independent kingdom with an ancient monarchy of its own and institutions that were not just clones of their English equivalents, as the Irish ones were, but had their own distinctive origins and traditions. In 1603, the play of dynastic marriage and inheritance brought a Stuart king to the throne of England. However, this did not bring about a union between the two countries. The only notable gesture towards union was a purely symbolic one: the laying of the St George's cross over the St Andrews saltire to create the Union Jack. But for a century it was only a royal standard and not a national one. Third, at the time of the Act of Union, Scotland was a

Protestant country. Except in parts of the Highlands, Catholic practice had disappeared even more completely than it had in England. From the sixteenth century until relatively recent times, Protestantism was at least as important as an element in Scotland's national identity as it was in England's. In 1688, England and Scotland both independently renounced their allegiance to James II because he was a Catholic, and invited the Dutch Stadholder William of Orange and his Stuart wife Mary to occupy the throne, because they had undertaken to secure the Protestant religion.

In spite of a common Protestant ideology, however, there was no emotional tide of British nationalism before the union of 1707, and no pressure for a union until shortly before it occurred. On the English side, the pressure for union arose from concerns about the defence of the realm very similar to those that prompted the union with Ireland a century later. After the Glorious Revolution of 1688, the exiled James II lived with his court at Saint-Germain under the patronage of Louis XIV of France, at a time of militant international Catholicism and major European wars. When James died, Louis XIV recognised his son as king of England. Jacobitism enjoyed considerable support in the Highlands and Islands, and elsewhere among the Episcopalians who had been ousted from the Church of Scotland. The risk of a French invasion through Scotland was taken extremely seriously at Westminster. But if defence was the main reason for a union in the eyes of the English, economic considerations were dominant among the Scots. They badly needed access to England's rapidly growing markets. The English domestic market was at least ten times the size of the Scottish one, and its colonial markets were more important still. The great engine of economic growth across much of eighteenth-century Europe was the raw materials and seaborne trade of the Americas and Asia. Yet this growth was very unevenly distributed as

European nations sought to reserve it to themselves. The Dutch, French and Spanish governments all reserved the trade of their colonies for the mother country.

In seventeenth-century England, the Navigation Acts reserved the colonial trade to English nationals and English ships. Scots were excluded from the right to trade with English colonies in Caribbean and North America. Attempts to break the monopoly were suppressed with growing efficiency by the English navy. Scotland was ill-placed to compete in this world of economic nationalism. It had a relatively small economy, with a limited range of exportable products, very little international clout and virtually no navy. Shortly before the union of 1707, Scotland's vulnerability was brought home to its inhabitants by the failure of an ambitious scheme of colonisation known as the Darien scheme. In 1695, Scotland chartered a company to found a colony at Darien on the Isthmus of Panama, in a region traditionally regarded as belonging to the sphere of influence of Spain. Under pressure from the English government, which wished to maintain good relations with Spain, English financiers refused to invest capital in it. As a result, the capital was ultimately subscribed by a large number of Scottish investors. The venture was a disaster, and by comparison with the modest size of the Scottish economy, the losses were enormous. They particularly affected the classes represented in the Scottish Parliament. There were a number of reasons for the failure of the scheme, including mismanagement, disease, Spanish hostility and absence of naval support. But the Scots blamed English indifference. In the years immediately leading up to the union of 1707, anti-English feeling in Scotland was probably stronger than it had been at any time since the Anglo-Scottish wars of the middle ages.

In 1704 the Scottish Parliament passed an Act reserving the right to choose a different monarch from England after the death of the childless Queen Anne, unless arrangements were made to secure 'the religion, liberty and trade of the nation from English or any foreign influence'. It was this overtly hostile enactment that led to the appointment of a joint commission to prepare a treaty of union. The passage of the Act of Union through the Scottish Parliament was eased by crude political horse-trading and a liberal distribution of bribes, and its enactment was accompanied by riots in Edinburgh, Glasgow and other towns. Rarely can a voluntary union have been agreed amid such a tide of mutual suspicion and resentment. Even after its passage there was a period of disillusionment during which a number of proposals were made for its repeal. One of them, in 1713, failed by only four votes in the House of Lords. In truth, when the Act of Union was passed, the common feeling of belonging which Renan identified as the foundation of nationhood did not exist. The union with Scotland had been the result of pragmatic calculations of mundane economic and political interest. The emergence of a wider British patriotism was a later development, the result rather than the cause of the union.

There is an interesting parallel to the situation of Scotland on the eve of the union, in the history of that other great imperial power, Spain. Spain came into being in its modern form as a result the dynastic union of the crowns of Aragon and Castile, when Ferdinand of Aragon married Isabella of Castile in 1479. As in Britain after 1603, it was a union of crowns but not a union of nations. Castile and Aragon retained their own distinctive institutions. But the Spanish colonial empire, which was run like the English one on strictly protectionist lines, was a purely Castilian affair. Catalans, traditionally the most dynamic traders among the subjects of the crown of Aragon, were excluded from the benefits of Spain's Caribbean and South American empire, just as the Scots were excluded before 1707 from England's

Caribbean and North American empire. As in Britain, the Catalans had no automatic access to Castilian domestic markets either. They paid duties at the boundary of Castile. As in Britain, this separation of Castile and Aragon ultimately proved to be intolerable because of the threat of foreign intervention. There was a powerful invasion of Catalonia from France in 1640, and another in 1705. But the solution was different. The problem was brought to an end not by a voluntary coalescence, as in England, but by forcible absorption. The whole process was a disaster for Catalonia, which atrophied economically for nearly two centuries. This was also the fate of eighteenth-century Ireland, which became an economic satellite of England; a source of raw materials, food and cheap labour. In Ireland, economic specialisation was limited. Urbanisation and manufacturing growth were slow. Capital formation was inhibited by the concentration of landed wealth in the hands of a largely non-resident aristocracy. By the beginning of the nineteenth century, industrialisation was actually going into reverse in Ireland, except in the Belfast area where substantially the whole of Irish heavy industry was to be concentrated for most of the next two centuries. The experience of eighteenth-century Scotland could hardly have been more different. After an uncertain start, the union brought spectacular economic benefits to Scotland. In the first century and a half after 1707, Scotland enjoyed a rate of industrialisation second only to England's own. Purely Scottish factors contributed much to this development: a relatively high standard of literacy and general education and a generous endowment of natural resources, particularly water power and coal. But by far the most important factor in the economic achievement of eighteenth-century Scotland was its new access to the domestic and international markets of England. Glasgow and the Clyde region became one of the major British centres of the transatlantic trades, and one of the greatest concentrations of heavy industry in the world. The men who built and managed these businesses were native Scots. The rapid expansion of the Scottish economy in the aftermath of the Act of Union was the most important single factor in the creation of a common British identity. But almost as important was a common belief in the Protestant settlement and the rhetoric of constitutional liberty, which were central to both nations' sense of identity.

Nations commonly identify themselves by comparison with some great other, and for both English and Scots, the great other was usually France. Britain was Protestant where the French were Catholic. Britain regarded itself as constitutionally free whereas the French were thought to be the servile helots of a privileged aristocracy and an absolute king. Britain thought of itself as rich and enterprising, while France stagnated as the riches of the land were appropriated by the few. It was to these stereotypes that the British ascribed their economic success and their remarkable imperial expansion in the eighteenth century. The frame of mind is perfectly encapsulated in William Hogarth's much reproduced painting *The Gate of Calais*, of 1748, in which starving and ragged Frenchmen are shown enclosed by a vast prison, pushed about by equally ragged soldiers, while in the background, well-fed Catholic monks live on the fat of the land. Appearing on American television in 2012, the then prime minister David Cameron was unable to identify the author of 'Rule Britannia'. For a convinced unionist, Mr Cameron was missing a trick. It was in fact written in 1745 by a Scot, James Thomson. This famous patriotic song was a great deal more than a celebration of British sea power. It was paeon of praise for political liberty, and a conviction that only in Britain was it to be found.

The nations, not so blest as thee,
  Must in their turn to tyrants fall,
While thou shalt flourish great and free,
  The dread and envy of them all.

Nothing promotes a sense of common patriotism as effectively as a common external enemy. In early eighteenth-century Britain, one of those enemies was Jacobitism. The threat of a Jacobite invasion of Scotland brought an insular, Protestant and British Scotland into conflict with a cosmopolitan Jacobite movement with its roots in international Catholicism and monarchical absolutism. The Stewarts may have been an authentically Scottish dynasty, but their refusal to abandon their Catholic faith made them foreign in the eyes of Britons on both sides of the border. At the outset of the Jacobite rebellion of 1715, the Old Pretender issued a proclamation declaring that once restored to the Scottish throne, he would repeal the Act of Union. A similar promise was made by his son, Bonnie Prince Charlie, in 1745. 'No Union' was one of the slogans carried on Jacobite banners in both rebellions. This proved to be a serious misjudgement. In the Lowlands, which accounted for almost all the population and wealth of Scotland, the Stuart Pretenders had little or no support, rather less in fact than they had in the north of England. The main result of the rebellions was to reinforce support for the union in most parts of Scotland. George II's Germanic younger son, William Duke of Cumberland, has gone down in history as the Butcher of Culloden, and the Highlanders whom he slaughtered have become symbols of a romanticised Scottish past. But at the time of the 'Forty-five', this quintessentially unScottish figure was a hero in Scotland. After the battle, he was elected Chancellor of the University of St Andrews and feted in the streets of Edinburgh. George II might have been a German who spoke poor English and never visited Scotland, but at least he was a Protestant. With the Stewarts laying claim to the British Crown, that was what mattered. Religious allegiance, which had been such a divisive factor in England's relations with Ireland, remained the cement of the union with Scotland for many years after the Jacobite threat had faded away. Even in the twentieth century, Protestantism remained part of the fabric of public life in Scotland in a way that had not been true of England for many years. The Presbyterian churches retained considerable political influence. Until half a century ago, those bastions of Scottish working-class culture, the Boy's Brigade, Sunday school and Rangers Football Club, were suffused with the ethic of muscular public Protestantism. If nations tend to define themselves by contrast with their neighbours, the Scots have historically defined themselves by contrast not with the English but with the Irish. The stereotyped image of the Irish as superstitious, primitive and feckless was a staple of political discourse in Scotland. The Scots were among the strongest opponents of Irish Home Rule at the end of the nineteenth century. Indeed, the Liberal Party's adoption of Irish Home Rule brought an end to the party's long-standing domination of Scottish parliamentary politics, as Scottish voters turned in droves to unionist parties.

The main shared experience of England and Scotland for the first two centuries of the union was the British colonial empire. The industries of the Clyde were heavily oriented towards the Atlantic trade, and later to the construction of the empire's infrastructure: shipbuilding, railway engines and harbour works. Scotland supplied a disproportionate number of the empire's imperial administrators and soldiers. They were among its most prolific and successful settlers, missionaries, engineers, traders and industrialists. In 1901, at a time when the Scots comprised about 10 per cent of the population of the United Kingdom, they made up about 15 per cent of the British-born population of Australia, 21 per cent in Canada and 23 per cent in New Zealand. There is some evidence that Scottish settlers in the colonies and dominions were not only more numerous but arrived with higher standards of education, more skills and more capital than other settlers from the British Isles. When the American steel baron Andrew Carnegie, who was born in Scotland, remarked that America would have been a poor show without the Scots, he had of course a vested interest. But he was not the only person who said so. The Irish politician Sir Charles Dilke, who toured the empire in the 1860s, observed that 'for every Englishman that you meet who has worked himself up from small beginnings, without external aid, you find ten Scotchmen'. The novelist Anthony Trollope, returning from Australia in the following decade, famously declared that 'in the colonies those who make money are generally Scotchmen and those who do not are mostly Irishmen'. The English tendency to praise the enterprise of the Scots while denigrating the Irish was perhaps as revealing as anything about their attitude to both of their British neighbours. It was a travesty in fact. There were large and prosperous Irish communities in North America, Australia and New Zealand. But it was true that, in proportion to their numbers, the Scots played a much larger part in the imperial operations of the British state than any other nation within the British Isles. Their activities as settlers contributed to the enrichment of their home country in a way that was not as true of the Irish or the English.

In much the same way, the Scots have played a remarkably prominent role in the government of the United Kingdom itself. For much of the eighteenth century the Scottish parliamentary block at Westminster produced few leaders, but succeeded in selling its support to the parliamentary managers of the Crown in return for a disproportionately large share of its patronage and influence. The eighteenth-century system of political patronage disappeared after the Reform Bill of 1832, but Scotland continued to have a weight in the government of the United Kingdom out of all proportion to its share of the British population. Of the thirty-two prime ministers who have held office since the 1850s, no fewer than eleven have been of Scottish ancestry and two more have sat for Scottish constituencies. The emergence of a specifically British patriotism was the result of the two centuries of shared experience of government, war, colonisation and industrialisation which followed the union. And by far the most important single factor behind such an emergence was the fact that the union occurred at the outset of the period of Britain's greatest international power and wealth, a process in which the Scots played an important part.

To return to the language of Ernest Renan, the English and Scots did great things together and until quite recently were intent on doing more. It is difficult to imagine that either would have been as successful in the heyday of British power without the other. What is striking about the rise of a specifically British patriotism in Scotland during the eighteenth and nineteenth century is not just that it happened, but that it proved to be entirely consistent with the survival of an authentic Scottish patriotism as well. The Scottish Parliament disappeared in 1707, and so, shortly afterwards, did the Scottish Privy Council, which had been the main organ of government north of the border. Until the creation of the Scottish Office in 1885, there were no government departments concerned specifically with Scotland. Even the Scottish Office was based in London until 1937. Yet the union left intact all of the indigenous institutions that were closest to the Scottish people. The Act of Union guaranteed the position of the Kirk as the established Church of Scotland, which came closest to being the authentic voice of Scotland in the next two centuries. It expressly preserved the Scottish judiciary, administering a body of Scottish law with its roots in continental civil law systems and differing in significant ways from the common law of England. It did not touch the Scottish school system or the four Scottish universities. Some of the most famous modern symbols of Scottish identity, such as kilts, sporrans, tartans and bagpipes, had been forbidden by statute after the Jacobite rebellion of 1745. But in the early nineteenth century they were readopted by a country by now largely urban and industrial, the population of which was concentrated in the Lowlands. Yet this recognition of a distinctive past existed side by side with a wider British nationalism. Ironically, the chief agents in the growing popularity of Scottish national dress in the nineteenth century were British institutions, notably the monarchy, which reinvented itself under Queen Victoria as a Scottish institution, and the War Office, which kitted out even the Lowland regiments in kilts and tartans. As the great Scottish historian of the Victorian age, Thomas Babington Macaulay, observed, every self-respecting Scot now went about wearing a costume that would once have been regarded as the authentic uniform of thieves and brigands.

A great deal has happened since 1707 to create a composite British nation out of the distinctive traditions of English and Scottish nationalism. The interesting question is why this counts for less now than it did only a generation ago. It is common to answer this question by referring to the well-advertised differences between Scottish politicians and the Conservative governments of the 1980s, and to the striking decline of the electoral fortunes of the Conservative Party in Scotland after a long period when it had been the dominant force in Scottish politics. But it is important not to confuse the symptoms with the cause. The most dramatic rise in the level of support for the Scottish National Party occurred in the first decade of the present century, at a time when the Labour Party was in power at Westminster, was led by Scots, and held a large majority of Scottish seats. This interesting phenomenon is likely to have had far more profound causes than the ephemeral issues that preoccupied British politicians at the time. In a sense the factors which have encouraged the decline of British nationalism are no more than the obverse of those that led to its creation in the first place.

The first and most obvious is the decline of Britain's sense of its own historic destiny and global relevance. This is a remarkable change that has occurred in the relatively short period since the Second World War, an event that marked perhaps the climactic moment of England's and Scotland's shared history. The British Empire was not the only European empire. But it was by far the largest of the European empires and it was the one the fortunes of which were most closely bound up with the identity of the nation that created it. Its disappearance has removed the principal historic experience that Scotland shared with England. It has also deprived Scotland, even more than England, of an outlet for emigration and a source of middle-class employment. The American political scientist Rogers Smith has suggested that every political community depends for its sense of identity on what he calls a 'constitutive story', a historical memory which explains who we are and why we belong together. This is in reality an updated and more elaborately argued version of Renan's theory of nationhood. In the last half-century, there has been a striking decline in Britain's confidence in the special value of its own collective experience. Take as an example the decline of English constitutional history. The struggles of the Crown and Parliament in the seventeenth century not only fed the eighteenth-century myths of national identity, but until quite recently seemed to be the paradigm for the development of constitutional liberty everywhere, a story of universal relevance. British constitutional history has all but vanished from the curricula of university history courses. Britain's overseas empire, which was a source of pride while it lasted, has become a matter for embarrassment and apology among many who have only the haziest idea of its history. When a state can no longer maintain its own constitutive story, Rogers Smith argues, historical memory becomes localised. This is what has happened in Britain. The last thirty years have witnessed a veritable explosion of interest in Scottish history, ranging from work of outstanding originality and scholarship to colourful fantasy and patriotic myth. Scotland is in the process of making its own constitutive story. In a world that is at the same time more globally minded and more locally minded, to be British seems less important.

Second, the institutions at the heart of Scottish life which contributed most to sustaining belief in the union in the eighteenth and nineteenth century have lost much of their influence. This applies particularly to those great engines of Scottish unionism, the British Army and the Scottish Kirk. For most of the history of the union, the British Army has been recruited in disproportionate numbers from north of the border. A quarter of the British Army at the battle of Waterloo fought in regiments raised in Scotland, at a time when only about one in seven of the population of the United Kingdom lived there. The role of Scottish troops as shock troops, generally deployed in the front line, meant that their casualties have always been high. In the First World War, Scottish regiments suffered casualty rates of about one in four, more than twice the average for the United Kingdom as a whole. All of this represented a highly visible contribution to a much admired and authentically British institution. The army has progressively contracted as Britain has shed its international responsibilities since 1945. The contraction has been particularly marked among the famous Scottish infantry regiments. As a result of successive suppressions and mergers, they have been reduced from eleven in 1957 to just one today, the Royal Regiment of Scotland.

The decline of the Kirk, that other notable bastion of unionism, has been a more complex and drawn-out process. The eighteenth and early nineteenth centuries were probably the high point of its influence. After the so-called Disruption of 1843, when the courts reaffirmed the rights of lay patrons in the Church of Scotland, some 40 per cent of the Kirk's membership seceded to form the Free Church. Although the social and political attitudes of the different Presbyterian churches were much the same, the established church lost much of its social pre-eminence and moral influence. Responsibility for poor relief was transferred from the Kirk to elected parochial boards in 1845. Education was transferred to elected bodies in 1872, with the introduction of universal, publicly funded elementary education. The urbanisation of Scotland inevitably weakened the grip of the Kirk on local government, since it never enjoyed the same influence over the municipal corporations of the expanding industrial cities as it had over the small towns and rural parishes. In 1929, even the Kirk's dominance of rural parochial councils was lost when these bodies were abolished. But since the Second World War, the progressive secularisation of British life on both sides of the border has transformed social attitudes to a degree that is hard for those brought up under modern conventions to grasp. Protestant church membership in Scotland has declined in half a century by more than two thirds. These changes have served to undermine the political influence of one the union's principal historic defenders, and put an end to the aggressive Protestantism that was once one of the major components of British national identity.

These changes have coincided with a broad range of social problems arising from the speed of Scotland's industrialisation in the nineteenth century, and of its de-industrialisation since the Second World War. These problems have affected the whole of the United Kingdom, but they have been more significant in Scotland, where steel, shipbuilding and heavy engineering in their heyday were a larger part of the economy and were more highly concentrated geographically. Perhaps the most notorious single symptom of Scotland's social problems was housing of the working classes, especially in the Clyde. Housing conditions in Glasgow were for many years the worst in Britain and among the worst in Europe. On the eve of the Second World War, one in four dwellings in Scotland was overcrowded according to the standard laid down in the Housing Act of 1935, as against only one in twenty-five dwellings in England. While the heavy industry of the Clyde prospered, a good deal of social amenity was sacrificed to feed its need for manpower. Yet in the 1930s, at a time of sluggish but steady growth in England, the Scottish economy was actually contracting, and in 1937 was smaller than it had been in 1913. After a pause resulting from the long post-war manufacturing boom, these divergences between England and Scotland resumed in the 1970s and 1980s. Between 1976 and 1987, Scotland lost nearly a third of its manufacturing capacity. Today, the differences have narrowed. The jobs have been replaced. Unemployment has generally been much the same in Scotland as in England. But there has been a shift away from traditional male working-class jobs in manufacturing, agriculture and construction, towards financial services, public services and tourism, all on a scale and at a speed much greater than the UK average.

The legacy of social dislocation resulting from both industrialisation and de-industrialisation has been addressed mainly by the expansion of the social action of the state in both England and Scotland. But the scale of the problems in Scotland was always likely to lead to a stronger commitment to governmental action there than in the rest of the United Kingdom. The Royal Commission on Housing in Scotland, the report of which was published in 1918, advised that the housing situation in western Scotland was so catastrophic that it could be addressed only by large-scale state intervention. At the time, this was an unpalatable message, with financial implications that the British state was unwilling to accept. Large-scale state intervention in the Scottish economy and society had to wait another quarter of a century. The turning point came in the 1940s with the Second World War and the major programme of state intervention inaugurated by the Labour government of 1945–51. In fact, parts of that programme had already been introduced in Scotland during the war years, as a result of the determination of the wartime coalition government to ensure the smooth operation of vital war industries located there. Tom Johnston, a Labour MP and secretary of state for Scotland in the wartime coalition, was given a free hand to promote his own brand of social action under powers derived from the vast apparatus of statutory wartime controls. Among Johnston's more notable monuments were rent review tribunals, the introduction of state-owned hydro-electric power to the Highlands and a sort of prototype national health service in the Clyde area. The post-war housing construction boom in Scotland was almost entirely the work of the public sector. In the two decades following 1945, public housing came to account for 86 per cent of new housing in Scotland, and even more in the Glasgow area. Looking at the position more broadly, in parts of western Scotland at the outset of the twenty-first century, public spending accounted for something like three quarters of the local economy. These were far higher proportions than could be found in any other part of the United Kingdom. They have inevitably had a profound effect on public attitudes to the state in Scotland, attitudes that differ significantly from the rather more equivocal view of the state taken by most Englishmen.

In a society heavily dependent for its well-being on state action, the remoteness of the directing organs of the state is likely to be resented. In a society that conceives itself to be different, and in important respects is different, the preference of governments for applying standard solutions across the board, and their impatience over regional differences, will provoke a sense of victimhood. All of these observable tendencies in complex societies are likely to be aggravated at a time of financial stringency, when public expectations of the state are likely to be disappointed anyway. These considerations may go some way to explain the outrage provoked in Scotland by the anti-state rhetoric of Mrs Thatcher's governments in the 1980s, and the attempts of both Conservative and Labour governments of the past four decades to rein in social spending. People who depend heavily on state action are likely to want to break down the organs of the state into smaller, more local and more responsive geographical units. When some of those units correspond to ancient polities like Scotland, with self-conscious identities of their own, the pressure to secede is strong.

The pressure for independence in Scotland has greatly increased as a result of the decision of the Labour government to hold a referendum on devolution in 1998 and, following a 74 per cent vote in favour, to establish a subordinate Parliament and Executive at Edinburgh with extensive devolved powers. The object was to contain Scottish nationalism by offering an alternative route to greater self-determination. In fact, it has had the opposite effect. The Scottish Parliament and Executive have been dominated for most of their history by the Scottish National Party. SNP governments have addressed some of the issues on which Scotland has an interest distinct from England's and a different political perspective. But they have also used their control over the devolved Parliament and government in Edinburgh to generate grievances against England, and to drive a wedge between the two principal nations of the United Kingdom in order to boost the cause of independence. This policy has been largely successful. Support for independence has substantially increased during their time in power.

The United Kingdom legislature conceded a referendum in 2014, and undertook to respect the result. This was in itself a remarkable decision. In no other European country would the government have reacted so calmly to the prospect of secession by a small but highly significant part of its population, with a common language and political tradition, which over a period of three centuries has participated in some of the greatest moments of its history. The United States fought a bitter civil war in the 1860s to prevent the secession of the Confederacy. The issue was not slavery, except perhaps at the very end of the civil war. It was the constitutional unity of the American state. Spain refused to allow a referendum on the independence of Catalonia in 2017 and attempted to prevent it from proceeding by force. It ultimately imposed direct rule from Madrid on Catalonia. A number of the political leaders of the independence movement have been convicted of sedition and jailed. The heavy-handed Spanish response was probably unwise, but the instinct behind it would have been shared by most European governments faced with a similar challenge. The more emollient English approach to the challenge of Scottish nationalism is in keeping with the pragmatic and unemotional considerations that brought about the union with Scotland in the first place. It fits in with the generally cooperative character of a union that has always been regarded as closer to an alliance than a merger of nations.

The Scottish independence referendum resulted in a narrow victory for the unionists. It was followed in 2016 by the referendum on the European Union, which resulted in an even narrower decision to leave the EU, and the United Kingdom has now left. The two referendums have both had a considerable impact on relations between England and Scotland. The independence referendum left two angry camps at each others' throats, as referendums tend to do. The EU referendum drove another wedge between England, which voted to leave by 59 to 41 per cent, and Scotland, which voted to remain by 62 to 38 per cent. Since 2016, opinion polls in Scotland have shown a small increase in support for independence, due mainly to a rise in support among those who voted to remain in the European Union. Support for independence is currently slightly above 50 per cent.

So what happens next? Legally, the United Kingdom holds all the cards. Independence is not an issue that has been devolved to the Scottish Parliament. It is reserved to the Parliament of the United Kingdom. A unilateral declaration of independence by the Scottish Parliament, after the manner of Catalonia, seems out of the question. It would probably not be tolerated by the Scottish judiciary and certainly not by third countries. Without international recognition Scotland would be unable, for example, to borrow on the international money markets, to let oil concessions offshore or to join the European Union. The Westminster Parliament has a solid unionist majority. The current Conservative government at Westminster has set its face against a second independence referendum. It is difficult to imagine a Labour government taking a different line. The Conservatives are unionists from conviction, the Labour Party from conviction allied to self-interest. Both have been badly hit by the rise of Scottish nationalism. But it is the Labour Party that has been the main loser. In Edinburgh and at Westminster it has been replaced as the party of the Scottish left by the Scottish National Party. The SNP currently holds 48 of the 59 Westminster seats in Scotland, and the Labour Party just one. The powerful position of the Conservatives in England has enabled them to control the government of the United Kingdom for most of the past century, with or without Scottish seats. The Labour Party is in a weaker position. It will find it exceptionally difficult to form a government in the United Kingdom without Scottish seats. This is a misfortune not just for the Labour Party at Westminster but for the cause of the union. England is a more conservative country than Scotland. The domination of the Scottish left by the SNP, and the shrinking prospect of a Labour government with an absolute majority at Westminster, threaten to provoke a long-term political schism between England and Scotland which can only increase the pressure for independence.

Against that background, is the British government's refusal to allow a second independence referendum sustainable? Politically it is sustainable for as long as there is a sufficiently determined unionist majority at Westminster. That may depend on whether it is morally and intellectually sustainable, which is a more difficult question. The UK government's position is that the Scots have had their referendum and that will do for a generation. This is not a defensible position and never could have been. Referendums are a snapshot of opinion. A decision in favour of independence would have been irrevocable, but a decision in favour of the status quo could never have been more than provisional. There is an additional reason why the referendum of 2014 could never have been decisive. It was fought on the basis that the United Kingdom was a member of the European Union and was likely to remain one. Both the plans of the nationalists and the opposition of the unionists depended on that. The

Scottish Nationalists are therefore right to say that the UK's departure from Europe creates a new situation.

But if the British government's argument against a second independence referendum does not amount to much, the same is true of the principal argument of the SNP in favour of one. Their position is that Scottish independence is just a matter for the Scots. On this view of the matter, the objections of a UK-wide Parliament at Westminster can have no legitimacy. This view is indefensible. The rejection of a second referendum by the Westminster government is legitimate for two fundamental reasons. The first is that the future shape of the United Kingdom is not just a matter for the Scots. It concerns the entire population of the United Kingdom. It is therefore a legitimate concern of the only Parliament that can be said to speak for the whole of the United Kingdom, namely the Westminster Parliament. The second reason is that as a national Parliament for the whole of the UK, the Westminster Parliament is both bound and entitled to take its own view of the interests of Scotland even if it differs from that of most Scots.

In his pamphlet, *England's Case against Home Rule*, published in 1886, A. V. Dicey addressed these questions in the context of the debates about Home Rule for Ireland. He argued that the shape of the United Kingdom was of equal concern to all of its citizens. The English, he thought, had as much right to decide whether the Irish should continue to be part of it as the Irish themselves did. Dicey was surely right about this. I have already cited Ernest Renan's famous lecture on what constitutes a nation. When Renan spoke of a nation as depending for its existence on collective sentiment, on a 'perpetual referendum' among its people, he begged the question: whose sentiment and which people? Such questions matter if you are proposing to sever an ancient nation. The major objection to the message of Scottish nationalism is its exclusivity. It involves a narrow-minded concentration on Scottish identity at the expense of every other aspect of the identity of people who have lived together in these islands in the same polity for three centuries. After three centuries of union, we are not just Scottish or English. We have migrated across the border in large numbers in both directions. There is a great Scottish diaspora in England and an English one in Scotland. We have moved in search of employment. We have intermarried. We have fought wars together as one country. We have an integrated economy. We have common social and economic challenges and will have more in future. Britain is a land of multiple identities. I am a Londoner, an Englishman and a Briton. As a Briton, Scotland is part of my country, just as Yorkshire or London is part of the heritage of every Scot. If the English were, hypothetically, to decide to constitute England and Wales as a separate country without Scotland, it would be absurd to suggest that the Scots were not entitled to a say. It is just as absurd to suggest that an irreversible decision to sunder Britain in two should be the sole prerogative of the 9 per cent of its population that lives in Scotland. Especially when that 9 per cent excludes the many Scots who live under the auspices of the union in England.

If the political and legislative organs of the United Kingdom are entitled to make a decision about Scottish independence, what might justify them in rejecting it? It would be unwise to reject it in the sole interest of England. But it would, as it seems to me, be entirely legitimate to reject it in the interest of the Scots or of the United Kingdom as a whole. Nations have interests extending beyond the opinions of the current generation. Because the consequences of Scottish independence would be irreversible, the Westminster Parliament is both bound and entitled to look to the long-term interests of Scotland as well as the rest of the United Kingdom. Its conclusions will not necessarily coincide with the snapshot view that the current inhabitants of Scotland may take in a referendum. Leaving aside (for the moment) the emotional dimension of Scottish nationalism, the case for independence in Scotland's interest is weak by any objective standard. Apart from defence and foreign policy, almost everything that an independent Scotland could do can be done by the Scottish government and parliament under the devolution regime. They do not need to be an international entity separate from the United Kingdom in order to give effect to their social or economic aspirations. Indeed, in a number of respects an independent Scotland would be less able to do so than it does now. The economic indicators are unfavourable. The outlook for oil prices, economically recoverable oil reserves, public revenues and disposable household income is poor – far worse than the assumptions made by the Scottish ministers at the time of the referendum of 2014. The departure of the United Kingdom from the European Union has added a good deal to the emotional charge of the independence movement, but it has also seriously undermined the economic case for Scottish independence. With the UK out of the European Union, an independent Scotland would be separated by a tariff barrier from a market that currently accounts for 60 per cent of its exports. This is a catastrophe in the making, whether the Scots recognise it or not. The reality is that we would all, Scots and English alike, be diminished by the secession of Scotland from the United Kingdom.

There are important lessons to be learned from both of Britain's recent experiments with constitutional referendums. One is that the emotional dimension of an issue like Scottish independence really matters. People are much more strongly influenced by emotion and identity than they are by economic facts and projections. They are also more attracted to upbeat and optimistic messages, however misleading, than they are to relentless forecasts of doom, especially economic doom. It is one of the ironies of the current situation that although Scottish nationalists have been forthright critics of the decision to leave the EU, the emotional arguments in favour of Scotland leaving the UK are remarkably similar to the emotional arguments in favour of the UK leaving Europe. They are just as obsessive, just as short-sighted, and just as mistaken, but they are also just as effective. This is because arguments based on emotion and identity go with the grain of human nature.

But it is also because both referendums were conducted on an artificial basis that made the economic issues easier to ignore. In both cases, the consequences of leaving were inevitably going to depend on the terms of departure. These were not known at the time of the vote because they would depend on the outcome of a difficult and complex future negotiation. In both cases extravagant claims were made by those who wanted to leave the larger entity about the terms that they would be able to negotiate. In neither case did people know what they were voting for. In the case of the decision to leave Europe, the terms actually available have proved to be very much less favourable than those forecast by leavers. It is almost certain that the same would have been true of a Scottish decision to leave the United Kingdom in 2014. This is why a referendum limited to the question of whether Scotland should be an independent state or the United Kingdom should be a member of the European Union is largely meaningless. The Europe referendum was the beginning, not the end, of the debate, because it resolved none of the major issues, all of which depended on the terms. It proved to be the starting gun for three and a half years of internal strife and a major constitutional crisis, which was resolved only by the election of a government committed to treating no deal as a serious option. No government or legislature mindful of the interests of either Scotland or England could wish on them such a thing. No deal became a serious option for England and the EU. It could never be a serious option for Scotland, because without a legislative dissolution of the Union at Westminster, Scotland cannot be independent. Agreement is therefore indispensable. If there is one thing that the aftermath of the Europe referendum should have taught us, it is that any referendum must be decisive of the issues. That means that if it is to be held at all, it must be held after and not before a contingent agreement has been reached on the terms. That would require a high level of statesmanship on both sides. But the importance of the issue requires nothing less.

I began this essay with an Act of Parliament. I want to end it with a work of fiction. In *A Farewell to Arms*, Ernest Hemingway's bleak novel of military life on the Italian front in 1917, there is an interesting exchange between the narrator's friend Rinaldi and the British nurse Helen Ferguson. 'You love England,' asks Rinaldi. 'Not too well,' comes the answer. And then, as if no other explanation was called for, 'I'm Scotch you see.' 'But Scotland is England,' says Rinaldi. 'Not yet,' said Miss Ferguson. 'Not really?' 'Never. We do not like the English.' 'Not like the English? Not like Miss Barklay,' says Rinaldi, referring to Helen's English friend. 'You mustn't take everything so literally,' she replies before breaking off the conversation.

In its original form, this was a lecture delivered at the Royal Geographical Society in February 2013, before the Scottish referendum of the following year and the EU referendum of 2016. I have updated the original text to reflect the outcome of these plebiscites and to consider the current situation.

LAW: CONCEPTIONS AND
MISCONCEPTIONS

6

HOME TRUTHS ABOUT
JUDICIAL DIVERSITY

In modern Britain, the fastest way to make enemies is to deliver a public lecture about judicial diversity. Unless you confine yourself to worthy platitudes, you are almost bound to cause offence to someone. It is of course quite possible to live a reasonably fulfilled life without thinking seriously about the subject at all. You can simply take the received clichés off the shelf. That was probably my position in 2006, when I became a member of the Judicial Appointments Commission upon its creation. I was of course aware that the whole issue of diversity was important, politically sensitive and controversial. But I had no particular preconceptions, apart from an instinctive feeling that the reasons for the domination of the judiciary by white males were complex, and that the selection process was probably no more than part of the problem. By the time I left the Commission in 2011, I had come to the rather depressing conclusion that the whole subject was bedevilled by an unthinking resort to sterile formulae and an unwillingness to ask awkward questions or address real dilemmas. This does no justice to an important and difficult issue that calls for a more honest and objective appraisal than it has usually received.

The judiciary has the same basic problem about diversity as many other British institutions. It is recruited on merit from a pool of highly educated and experienced legal practitioners. This pool is itself dominated by white males, for reasons that have deep roots in our history and culture. The problem begins with an educational system that tends to perpetuate disadvantage. It continues with patterns of working in ancient professions, and with unspoken, often unconscious attitudes that have been many years in the making. The Bar has existed in one form or another for more than seven centuries. Helena Normanton, the first woman to practise as a barrister, was called just ninety years ago. Attitudes have changed. But the legacy of the past will take a long time to disappear.

The basic facts will be familiar to all of us. Currently (2020), 32 per cent of the judiciary of England and Wales are women compared with 51 per cent of the population at large, and 7 per cent are from ethnic minorities compared with 12 per cent of the population at large. The proportion of both women and ethnic minority office-holders is at its highest in the lower reaches of the judiciary, among district judges, masters, registrars, costs judges and deputy holders of these offices. It then tails off as one moves up the judicial hierarchy. The proportion of women on the High Court bench, at 28 per cent, is close to their proportion in the judiciary as a whole, but the number of ethnic minority judges is less satisfactory. It is 4 per cent. There are two women on the Supreme Court. These figures represent the current state of play. But it is not a static situation. The proportion of women in the judiciary has more than doubled since 1998, and the proportion of ethnic minority office-holders has trebled. To some extent, these trends are due to a stronger awareness of diversity as an issue among those responsible for selecting judges. But for the most part, it is the natural consequence of the progressive increase in the proportion of female and ethnic minority practitioners entering the legal profession since the 1960s. As these people move to the top of their profession, they represent a larger proportion of the pool available for judicial office. One would expect the results to be reflected in the appointments, and by and large they are. The regular series of statistics published by the Judicial Appointments Commission suggest that although there are fewer applications from women than from men, the proportion of female applicants shortlisted and the proportion selected are converging with the corresponding proportions for men. In the case of ethnic minority candidates, the degree of convergence is smaller. However, even critics of the current system generally accept that in the long term a judiciary broadly representative of the population at large will come about. The problem is not the direction of change. It is the speed. Human beings have a touching confidence in the capacity of their institutions to decree immediate changes, when in fact all that they can do is push them in the right direction.

I want to examine the reasons for the relatively slow progress towards a more diverse judicial bench, and the arguments for and against a measure of positive discrimination in the appointments system. This is a debate that matters, because positive discrimination is, I believe, the only thing that is likely to accelerate the rate of progress significantly. It does not of course follow that positive discrimination is desirable, and I shall explain why in my view it is not. But it should at least be on the agenda.

The starting point for any serious analysis of the current state of affairs is the statutory criteria for the appointment of judges. These broadly reflect the criteria that had been applied for years by the Lord Chancellor before 2006. The present position is that under Section 63(2) of the Constitutional Reform Act 2005, the Judicial Appointments Commission is required to make selections 'solely on merit'. Apart from the overriding requirement that those selected should be of good character, merit is the only criterion permitted by the Act. The Act does not define merit. But it does make it perfectly clear that merit is a criterion for assessing competing candidates for selection. It refers to their relative ability to perform the functions that will be required of them if they are appointed. This embraces a wide range of personal and intellectual characteristics, as well as public expectations about how judges should behave. But the essential point is that under the statute, merit is a characteristic of the individuals selected. The concept of merit does not allow candidates to be selected with a view to altering the make-up of the judiciary as a whole. Of course, the balance of qualities required by the judiciary as a whole is relevant for some purposes. It is, for example, perfectly legitimate under the current legislation to select candidates with an eye to achieving a proper balance between, say, chancery specialists and criminal lawyers, or between commercial lawyers and general common lawyers. But this approach is simply not available when it comes to achieving a satisfactory balance between men and women or between different ethnic groups. The difference is that if there is a special need for, say, chancery or family practitioners, then experience of chancery or family work is relevant to a candidate's ability to do the job better than a competing candidate. Racial identity or gender are not relevant to a candidate's ability to do the job. Indeed, it is a fundamental premise of our law on discrimination that they should not be treated as relevant. As the law presently stands, therefore, the Judicial Appointments Commission is not allowed to select a candidate over the head of a competent competitor on the ground that his or her presence on the bench would improve the gender or ethnic make-up of the judiciary as a whole.

The point is reinforced by the next section of the Act, Section 64. Section 64 was loosely modelled on the corresponding provisions of the legislation governing judicial appointments in Northern Ireland. It requires the commission to 'have regard to the need to encourage diversity in the range of persons available for selection for appointments'. It is confined to the composition of the pool of candidates from which selections are made. It is also expressly made subject to the obligation to select solely on merit in Section 63. So the scheme of the Act is tolerably clear. The commission's duty is to do its best to encourage applications from the widest possible range of eligible candidates, including those from non-traditional backgrounds. Having done that, it must select among them according to their relative aptitude for the job and nothing else. The record of the debates and committee proceedings during the passage of the Act through Parliament leaves no doubt that this was deliberate. There were two schools of thought among parliamentarians, sometimes referred to as the 'minimalist' and the 'maximalist' schools. Put crudely, the minimalist position was that the function of a selecting authority was to identify those who were good enough to do the job, and then to choose from among them in accordance with wider criteria. These wider criteria would have included the desirability of a judiciary that was as far as possible as diverse as the population at large. The maximalist position was that the selecting authority should choose candidates who are not just good enough, but the best available irrespective of race, gender, professional background, or any other consideration. The maximalists prevailed in the drafting of the criteria for selection. But the government introduced Section 64 by amendment during the passage of the bill through the House of Lords. The effect was to introduce diversity as part of the commission's duty in relation to the composition of the pool of candidates but not in relation to the criteria for selection.

More recently, the statutory criterion has been supplemented by section 159 of the Equality Act 2010, the so-called tie-breaker clause. The effect of section 159 is that as between candidates who are equally qualified for the job, preference may lawfully be given to the one whose appointment would contribute to rectifying the under-representation of some disadvantaged category. Ambitious claims have been made for the tie-breaker clause. This is unfortunate, because its effect is likely to be limited. A practice corresponding to the tie-breaker was applied by the Judicial Appointments Commission for most of the five years that I was a commissioner. But it depends for its operation on there being a tie, and ties are not as common as you might think. In any large selection exercise, the usual pattern is that most candidates will be bunched together in the middle of the ability range. They will be difficult to arrange in merit order. Many of them will be genuinely tied. But at the upper end of the ability range, there is usually clear water between every candidate once one looks at them in detail.

When the Judicial Appointments Commission started work in 2006, there was a strong political expectation that its creation would result in the immediate acceleration of our progress towards a more diverse judiciary. This did not happen, at any rate straight away. As a result, the commission came under a certain amount of public criticism and faced strong political pressures to speed things up. However, no convincing case has ever been made that there was an implicit bias either in the commission's procedures or in the way that it applied them. The most vocal critics simply pointed to the high proportion of white males, as if it necessarily followed that they were not the best candidates. The more thoughtful critics have usually pointed to the role played in it by consultees and referees, who are commonly existing judges. A French judge once said to me: of course hardly any judges are women in England; they are chosen by co-option by the existing judges, who are men. You sometimes hear the same rather crude notion expressed in England. I think that there was some limited truth in it in the days when candidates were tapped on the shoulder by the Lord Chancellor. This was because the Lord Chancellor's Department depended almost entirely on information supplied by judges in order to know who was worth considering. I do not believe that the judges were out to clone themselves then, any more than they are now. But it would be foolish to pretend that they were not occasionally influenced by unconscious stereotyping and by perceptions of ability moulded by their own personal experience. The absence of any wider sources of information made this very difficult for the appointments staff in the Lord Chancellor's Department to control. After 1995, the appointments system was progressively opened up to applications, and for nearly a decade now all appointments have been applications-based. The result has been that information is available to selectors from a much wider range of sources.

The influence of the existing judiciary has been correspondingly diluted. But it has not been eliminated, and nor should it be. Judges once appointed are difficult, and in the case of the High Court and above, almost impossible to remove. It cannot be right to make appointments simply on the basis of the information that candidates give about themselves, or on assessments made in the course of interviews and role-plays. The information that candidates give about themselves is inevitably selective, sometimes tendentiously so. Interviews are only a snapshot. They are unduly affected by the candidate's mood on the day and more generally by his or her interview skills. It cannot be in the public interest to marginalise or ignore the views of those such as professional judges, who have personal experience of doing the job and often have direct knowledge of a candidate's qualities or defects extending over many years. I would not deny that traditional stereotypes are a factor in some consultation responses and references, but I have to say that I saw little evidence of it in the five years that I spent reading these things. The JAC makes it perfectly clear in the material sent to referees and consultees what is expected of them. They are expected to give reasons for their views. Their influence is directly proportionate to the quality of those reasons, which is generally high. Under the current system, they can be and are tested against other sources of information. The Judicial Appointments Commission has a majority of lay members and a lay chair. Its assessment panels generally have one judicial member but a lay majority.

Of course the Judicial Appointments Commission is fallible like all human institutions. But by and large it does a difficult job about as well as it can be done. The main problem which the commission has faced is that the high expectation that it would bring about a sudden acceleration of the rate of diversification was simply unrealistic. It was based on the mistaken belief that the lack of diversity in judicial appointments was due to the failings of the selection process previously operated by the Lord Chancellor's Department. The statutory criteria which the Judicial Appointments Commission was required to apply in selecting judges were exactly the same as those that had been applied by the Lord Chancellor for years: in other words, selection on merit alone. According to the 2003 consultation paper on judicial appointments, what was needed to improve the diversity of the bench was 'a major re-engineering of the process for appointment'. In other words, the whole issue was approached on the basis that it was all just a question of procedural engineering. Implicit in this idea was the assumption that there was a large untapped reserve of potential talent among women and ethnic minorities, comprising people who were at least as good as those who were actually being appointed, but who had been overlooked or devalued by the Lord Chancellor's Department. It followed that this had only to be corrected for the benefits to become apparent.

This was a very crude analysis of a complicated situation. But it was unintentionally encouraged by the assertion, constantly reiterated by politicians, senior judges and even occasionally by spokesmen for the commission itself, that the achievement of a fully diverse judiciary was entirely compatible with selection on merit. Over the long term this is undoubtedly true. The ambition and talent required for a career leading to appointment as a judge is randomly distributed throughout the population. It is not the preserve of any one gender or ethnic group. It follows that selection on merit alone can be expected eventually to produce a diverse judiciary. But it will happen only over a considerable period of time. In the short term, accelerated progress towards a diverse judiciary is not going to be achieved under a system of appointment on merit alone. It is a question of timing. This is the major source of unrealistic expectations, and therefore of disappointment in the outcome.

Without some kind of positive discrimination, the judiciary is never going to be significantly more diverse than the pool from which it is drawn. The pool from which it is drawn is not the population at large, but the legal profession. The main reason for the lack of diversity in the English bench is the undiverse character of the upper reaches of the legal profession. To be eligible for most judicial appointments, you must have been a practising lawyer for a minimum period of time, generally five or seven years. In practice, almost all candidates have many more years than this. There are two obvious reasons why applicants for the more senior posts are always likely to come from the top end of the profession. One is that the ablest practitioners are reluctant to apply when they are young. They tend to enjoy their profession and will only leave it when they have got as far in it as they think they can, or feel like a change. The other is that long professional experience in a candidate provides selectors with the evidence that is required in order to make an object-ive assessment. Not all of those who are appointed to the bench will have been good advocates at the bar or outstand-ing legal scholars. But almost all of them will have been able to point to a sustained track record of personal and profes-sional achievement.

Currently (2020), 38 per cent of self-employed practising barristers are women but only 16 per cent of QCs. Exclud-ing those whose ethnicity is not recorded, ethnic minorities accounted for 14 per cent of the self-employed bar but only 8 per cent of QCs. I am concentrating on the self-employed bar, because it is the pool from which the great majority of applicants for the higher judicial offices come. For a variety of historical and practical reasons, the proportion of solici-tors experienced in the work of the courts is small, and the proportion interested in becoming judges smaller still. But it is right to point out that the corresponding figures for women solicitors are not much better than those for the bar. For most of the last twenty-five years, a majority of those passing the solicitors' final examinations have been women. Currently, women account for 49 per cent of solicitors but only 33 per cent of partners of firms. Attrition rates for women in both branches of the legal profession are high. Across the board, earnings, which are probably a fair reflection of professional opportunities, were significantly lower for women than for men.

The reasons for this pattern are beyond the scope of this essay. Clearly, one of them is the time required to reach the top. As more women reach the top of the profession, the pool of candidates for judicial appointment will become more diverse. This can also be expected in the long term to diminish the effect of gender stereotyping which is chiefly responsible for the unconscious prejudice that many women and ethnic minority practitioners still encounter among colleagues and clients. However, although time will heal some of these barriers to professional advancement, it will not heal all of them. The major barrier to the professional advancement of women has been identified by the surveys commissioned over the years by the Law Society and the Legal Services Commission. It is the exceptional demands that the profession makes on its most successful practitioners, in terms of commitment, working conditions and sheer hours. Not everyone wants to put up with this. Those who do not are making a perfectly legitimate lifestyle choice. Only the equal sharing of household and childrearing obligations between men and women can be expected to have a significant effect on this critical aspect of the culture of the professional workplace. It may happen, but it will involve a very profound long-term change in social attitudes, which is beyond the reach of legislation and is, as yet, just beginning. Studies carried out in other jurisdictions suggest that these problems are by no means peculiar to England. They are common to almost all western societies.

Perhaps the most striking way to illustrate the impact of working conditions in the legal profession on judicial diversity is to compare the experience of England with that of a jurisdiction in which judges are not recruited from the practising legal profession. France, like most civil law countries, has a career judiciary. Almost all judges embark upon a judicial career in their twenties with a period of training in the Ecole Nationale de la Magistrature, followed by an appointment at the age of twenty-five to thirty to an entry-level judicial position. There is a procedure for lateral recruitment of candidates at a later stage of their careers, but the numbers involved are small and they tend to come not from independent practice but from the academic world. The impact of this system on ethnic diversity is impossible to assess, owing to the long-standing French taboo against collecting ethnically classified data. But the figures for gender diversity are very remarkable. A majority of French judges have been women for many years. The proportion has risen rapidly over the last four decades, and is currently (2020) 67 per cent. This is an average over the whole judiciary. The proportions vary according to the sector. In some sectors, notably civil courts of first instance and family courts, the proportions are much higher. The proportions in the upper reaches of the judiciary (the so-called *hors-hierarchies*) are less impressive. But they are a good deal higher than they are at the corresponding level in England. They are likely to go on rising rapidly, because the pool from which candidates for appointment are drawn is dominated by women. Currently, more than 83 per cent of newly qualified graduates emerging from the Ecole National de la Magistrature are female.

The French experience suggests that where women can become judges without having to go through the ordeals of private legal practice, many more of them will want a judicial appointment and will get it. The procedures for selection and promotion of judges in France are rigorously based on merit. The powerful position of women in the French judiciary certainly suggests that whatever may be the cause of the glass ceiling that retards the progress of women to the top jobs, it is unlikely to be male prejudice or gender stereotyping. The consensus in France is that the most important single factors are career breaks for childrearing and the greater difficulty that women experience in moving to another part of the country to take up a more senior judicial post. However, to an outsider like me and to quite a few insiders as well, the French situation seems just as unsatisfactory as our own, albeit for different reasons. The major factor behind the rising proportion of women embarking on a judicial career in France has been the increasing reluctance of men to contemplate a judicial career. Only about 16 per cent of those sitting the final examinations of the Ecole Nationale de la Magistrature are men. The evidence is that in a world where professional and judicial careers are separate streams with very little in the way of transfer between them, men will opt disproportionately for professional practice. This is thought to be because it is perceived to bring higher financial rewards, greater independence, and more status than the judiciary, at a cost in terms of hours and working conditions which men are more willing to pay than women are. On the assumption, which seems reasonable, that men are just as capable of being judges as they were fifty years ago when 93 per cent of French judges were male, the current situation results from an artificial reduction in the pool from which judges are chosen by the wholesale withdrawal of men. This is not in the public interest and is no more compatible with a diverse judiciary than our own situation.

In England, the recruitment of judges from the higher ranks of the legal profession has, on the whole, served us well. It has generated a culture in which many of the ablest lawyers of their generation have come to regard judicial appointment as the culmination of a successful professional career. It has produced a judiciary of outstanding intellectual calibre and broad legal experience. It is a significant contributory cause of the highly developed sense of judicial independence among English judges. These are particularly important considerations in a system such as ours in which judges have a higher public profile and a larger role in the making of law than their civil law counterparts. However, the price that we have paid for these advantages is a less diverse judiciary than exists in most of Europe. We are simply deluding ourselves if we try to pretend that selection from legal practitioners on merit alone will produce a fully diverse, or even a reasonably diverse judiciary quickly. It will happen, but it will take a long time. The average judicial career lasts for more than twenty years. It follows that even if a rigid quota system were to be introduced tomorrow morning requiring the appointment of women and ethnic minority candidates in proportions exactly matching their presence in the population at large, something that no one is suggesting, it would still take fifteen or twenty years to achieve a fully diverse judiciary. As it is, it seems certain to take much longer. Recent forecasts suggest that under the current system and on current trends it may take fifty years.

The irony is that if the Lord Chancellor had retained the power to select judges, instead of passing it to the Judicial Appointments Commission in 2006, he could, and I suspect would, have treated diversity as a criterion for appointment. He would probably have done this with the minimum of fuss and without acknowledging publicly that he was doing it. The result would have been a somewhat faster rate of progress towards a diverse bench. However, the Lord Chancellor made appointments in the exercise of the prerogative power of the Crown. He was not bound by any statutory criteria, apart from the minimum period of legal qualification. Within the broad limits of rationality, he could do more or less as he liked. Even if he had gone badly wrong, the opacity of his processes would have made his selections difficult to challenge. The Judicial Appointments Commission is not in the same position. It has to apply statutory criteria for selection. Its procedures are published and they are relatively transparent. It records every stage of each selection exercise, and the record is subject to review by the Judicial Appointments and Conduct Ombudsman. It could not fudge or cheat even if it wanted to. Some people have regretted the change for that reason. But I doubt whether a discreet change of practice by the Lord Chancellor could ever have been the right way of achieving a significant alteration in this important area of public policy. If our society wants to achieve a faster move to diversity than is consistent with selection on merit from the existing pool, it can do it. But it should be done overtly by amending the statutory criteria for selection, after a proper public debate about the wider implications. It should not be done covertly by a minister.

We need, as a society, to have an honest public debate about the hitherto unmentionable subject of positive discrimination. We have to decide whether we want to accept a measure of positive discrimination in the selection of judges, as the price of making faster progress towards judicial diversity. There are arguments both for and against it. But the real problem is that the debate has not happened. It has not happened because of the conventional assumption that merit and diversity are compatible, even in the short term. This assumption enables us to pretend that the issue does not arise, that it is just a question of selecting on merit in a more intelligent way. Because we are not prepared to recognise that selection on merit is only compatible with a move to a diverse bench over a considerable period of time, we have never thought seriously enough about the choice to be made between them. I doubt whether we can afford to tiptoe round these issues for much longer.

So what is the case for positive discrimination?

However one looks at it, there are in reality three reasons why one might legitimately regard the present situation as unsatisfactory and want to see it changed quickly. The first is that if women and ethnic minorities comprise a much smaller proportion of judges than they do of candidates, one has to ask whether this is due to a failure in the selection process. I have already given my reasons for believing that the process is in fact careful, fair and meritocratic, as the statute requires it to be. That leaves two substantial arguments. One is that justice is administered better by a diverse judiciary. The other is that public belief in the legitimacy of the judiciary depends at least in part on the symbolic impact of its being staffed with people who are recognisably representative of society at large. These are not usually presented as arguments in favour of positive discrimination. But that is on analysis what they are. Both arguments are saying that we ought to be looking not only at the relative merits of individual candidates for the job, but at the merits of different possible compositions of the judiciary as a whole. On this view, the best possible judiciary may not necessarily be the one that contains all of the best available individuals. I do not myself accept either of these arguments, for reasons that I will explain. But they are both supported by distinguished and experienced voices.

Does a diverse bench administer justice differently or better? A great deal of research has been done on this subject, almost all of it in the United States. Some of it has been cited in the literature on judicial diversity in England, on the assumption that its conclusions may have a broader application. I cannot claim to have read all of this material. But I have read a lot of it and I have to say that I have found it rather unenlightening. Broadly speaking, most of it seeks to establish a statistically significant connection between the colour or gender of judges and the likelihood of a 'liberal' or a 'conservative' outcome. The criteria used for identifying any particular outcome as 'liberal' or 'conservative' seem to me to be rather crude, even as applied to the areas of civil rights, discrimination and penal policy on which most of the research has concentrated. Moreover, most of it makes no, or very little, allowance for the possibility that the outcome, however classified, may actually be attributable to the facts of individual cases or the state of the law, rather than to the gender or ethnicity of the tribunal. Even so, most of this substantial body of work is inconclusive. The general tenor of the rest is that in politically charged cases the most significant influence on outcomes in these cases is the political affiliation of the president or state governor by whom the judges in question were appointed. Race appears to have no discernible effect on outcomes, and gender only a very slight one. Some but not all researchers claim to have detected a greater propensity on the part of panels with at least one female member to prefer 'liberal' outcomes in discrimination or civil rights cases and 'conservative' outcomes in criminal cases. I have serious doubts about the value of this work even in the United States. I do not think that it transfers easily to a jurisdiction such as ours where there is a strong judicial culture of political neutrality and judicial appointments have not been influenced by political affiliation since the Second World War.

A more moderate, and to my mind more persuasive approach has been proposed by the former Chief Justice of Canada, Beverley MacLachlin, when addressing the issue of gender equality. She has distanced herself, surely rightly, from the view that women judge differently from men, or come to the business of judging with different ethical preconceptions. In a lecture delivered in Sydney, Australia, in 2006, she pointed out that this view overstated gender differences.

> In fact, men and women are diverse, come from different cultural and social backgrounds and possess a variety of values. To suggest a single feminine world view discounts the incredible variety and diversity of women … We are all trained jurists, and when we apply the law and common sense, we are likely to come to the same conclusions irrespective of gender.

However, Chief Justice McLachlan argues that the quality of justice is nevertheless improved by a diverse bench for a more subtle reason, namely that a diverse judiciary is able to draw on a wider range of collective experience.

> Jurists [she says] are human beings and, as such, are informed and influenced by their backgrounds, communities and experiences. For cultural, biological, social and historic reasons, women do have different experiences than men. In this respect women can make a unique contribution to the deliberations of our courts. Women are capable of infusing the law with the unique reality of their life.

I have the strongest doubts about this argument. In the first place, it can only apply to judicial decisions by multi-member panels operating in a collegiate fashion. In this country, that means the Supreme Court, the Court of Appeal, and certain tribunals and magistrates courts. Single judge courts, which make the great majority of judicial decisions, are by definition undiverse. Second, I think that it overstates the importance of personal as opposed to vicarious experience. No judge, from whatever background he or she may come, can ever claim personal experience of more than a tiny proportion of the situations that he or she is called upon to consider. Most judicial experience is necessarily vicarious and always will be. It is derived from intelligent social observation, and a sensitive empathy with those who find themselves in situations that the judge is unlikely to have experienced. I do not doubt that men and women have experiences of life that differ in some respects. But I deny that because a particular kind of experience is specific to one gender, judges of a different gender cannot comprehend it. The image of the inward-looking, out-of-touch judge is a journalistic cliché, and it is no doubt true of a few judges. But as a generalisation it is manifestly false. We quite rightly expect judges to understand the position of, for example, asylum seekers, immigrants, and other socially disadvantaged categories, without personal experience of being in their position. The case law amply demonstrates that they do. Judges ought not to have personal experience of committing crimes. But an understanding of the position of those who do commit them is required of every judge who is called upon to hear a plea in mitigation or receive a social enquiry report. Family judges are daily required to understand a wide range of gender-specific concerns of both spouses, although the judge can share the gender of only one of them. In *Radmacher v. Granatino*, the Supreme Court decision on the legal significance of prenuptial agreements, Baroness Hale observed in a dissenting judgment that there was a gender dimension to the question, because of the possibility that prenuptial agreements could become an instrument of oppression. She famously asked whether such an issue was suited to decision by a court comprising eight men and one woman. My own provisional answer to that question would be Yes. It is just as suitable for decision by a court with a majority of men as the many earlier cases in which all-male panels of the Court of Appeal or the House of Lords recognised the vulnerability of women in a relationship commonly dominated by men. The doctrine of presumed undue influence and the deserted wife's equity in the matrimonial home are both principles of law devised for the protection of women by all-male courts. The same is true of most of the seminal decisions made by white male judges over the last forty years that have reinforced the statutory protection against gender and race discrimination. And I would say that it is equally true of the careful and impartial women judges at every level who daily deal with the emotional and material problems that matrimonial break-up poses for men.

Quite apart from the lack of any empirical evidence, there are other objections to the notion that a diverse court produces a higher quality of justice. If personal experience of belonging to a relevant group is desirable, there will be very many relevant groups apart from women and ethnic minorities who are entitled to be represented. Even among women and ethnic minorities, there will be countless sub-groups, each with their own particular and relevant experience. Should we distinguish between ethnic minorities according to whether they are of Caribbean, African, Indian or Chinese origin, or between Christian, Muslim and Hindu, all categories with a unique quality of personal experience? If vicarious experience of life is not good enough, then how far should we go in ensuring that disputes are referred to judges with some relevant personal experience? How far can one go in this direction without undermining the objectivity of the judge, which necessarily depends on a certain personal distance from the facts? Ultimately, the emphasis on personal judicial experience of diverse social groups leads to the fragmentation of the judicial function. It leads to an attitude of mind that treats appellate courts as a sort of congress of ambassadors from different interest groups. I cannot be alone in regarding this as a travesty of the judge's role.

I turn to the other argument in favour of positive discrimination, which is based on concerns about the lack of legitimacy of an undiverse bench in the eyes of the wider public. In principle, I accept this. I think, however, that it is unfortunate. The call for more members of particular groups on the bench is a symptom of the fragmentation of our society. It is influenced by a widespread belief that judicial decisions are vitiated by the social ignorance of judges, or by their tacit loyalty to their class, gender, race or other constituency, or by inescapable social conditioning. I regard this belief as profoundly mistaken. I think that it is also unrealistic. Whoever they are and however recruited, judges as a group will never be representative of the public at large. Even in a fully diversified system, we would continue to expect our judges to have outstanding intellectual and personal qualities which will necessarily mark them out from the average. But the existence of a widespread feeling that an undiverse bench lacks legitimacy ought to be a source of concern whether or not we happen to agree with it. The judiciary has immense power. In the nature of things, judges cannot be democratically accountable for their decisions. It therefore matters very much that their role should be regarded as legitimate by the public at large. Legitimacy depends on collective sentiment. It cannot be analysed exclusively in rational terms. There has never been a sufficiently comprehensive and carefully designed survey of public attitudes to the judiciary to enable firm conclusions to be drawn about this. But there are certainly significant groups who question the legitimacy of an undiverse bench in modern social conditions, and their view is increasingly shared by the public. What remains entirely unclear is whether the public would still take this view if they appreciated that faster progress towards a diverse judiciary would require the partial abandonment of selection on merit. This is a real dilemma.

In any honest debate about positive discrimination, we would need to measure the advantages of a more representative judiciary against a realistic assessment of the cost of achieving it. In particular, we need to make some assessment of the impact on the quality of the bench that would result from qualifying the principle of selection 'solely on merit'. Because we have so far managed to persuade ourselves that the question does not arise, very little research has been done on this question either. But however much research was done on it, the answer would probably always be at least partly a matter of informed impression. My own, I hope informed, impression is that the impact on the quality of the bench would be serious.

There are several reasons why making diversity a criterion for appointment would adversely affect the quality of appointments. Self-evidently, if you dilute the principle of selecting only the most talented candidates by introducing criteria other than individual merit, you will by definition end up with a bench on which there are fewer outstanding people. But there is a more serious problem even than that. It is the impact that the change would have on applications. The quality of judicial appointments is highly sensitive to the quality of applicants. The qualities required for appointment to the bench, particularly at the more senior levels, are relatively rare. Those who possess them are in the nature of things likely to have many alternative opportunities open to them. Most of those opportunities will be a great deal more remunerative. Quite a few will also be more interesting and enjoyable than many judicial appointments. Practice at the upper reaches of the bar or a solicitor's firm is intellectually highly satisfying. Successful practitioners will usually have a more varied and challenging diet of work than most first-instance judges. Even the Court of Appeal has to deal with a fair amount of mundane business that would rarely if ever come the way of an experienced QC or litigation solicitor. Nevertheless, as matters stand, very large numbers of outstanding candidates do apply for judicial appointment, and it is important to understand why they do. First, they are attracted by the judiciary's collective reputation, which is heavily dependent on the principle of selection on individual merit. Second, there is a strong culture of public service in the legal professions. It is easy to scoff about this. But it is a matter of daily experience that highly qualified candidates are willing to accept judicial appointment, even though it is not in their financial interest, and even though judicial life is often less agreeable than the alternatives. Third, there is the tradition, which is particularly important at the bar, that judicial appointment is the ultimate accolade of a successful career. These things are very much in the public interest. They have made a contribution to the quality of the judiciary that would be hard to overstate. But like all human arrangements founded on convention and sentiment, this is a fragile construct. Once undermined, it will not easily be recreated. Outstanding candidates will not apply in significant numbers for judicial appointments if they believe that the appointment process is designed to favour ethnic or gender groups to which they do not belong. They will not walk away out of pique. They will walk away because the qualification of the principle of appointment on merit will have undermined much that makes judicial office attractive to outstandingly able people. Judicial appointments which are not made 'solely on merit' will lack the prestige in their eyes that was previously due to the assumption that only the best people get appointed. There will quite simply be better things for the most attractive candidates to do. Few constituencies would be more seriously affected by this than women and ethnic minorities. Positive discrimination is patronising. Those women and ethnic minority candidates who have been appointed under the current system are justifiably proud of having achieved this under a system based exclusively on individual merit. Many, probably most of those who are not judges but aspire to be appointed, do so because the principle of selection on individual merit makes it an ambition worth achieving. A partial abandonment of that principle would therefore be likely to make judicial office a great deal less attractive to the very people that its proponents are trying to help.

I do not expect everyone to agree with the views that I have expressed. In any event those views are necessarily provisional, for there remains much that we do not know and cannot foresee. What I hope I have demonstrated is that the whole subject of judicial diversity is an exceptionally complex and delicate issue, in which crude slogans, easy clichés and simple policy prescriptions are likely to have unintended and damaging side effects. They are likely to undermine much that is good about our current system, without necessarily curing what is bad about it. In this area, as in life generally, we cannot have everything that we want. We have to make choices and to accept impure compromises. We may even have to learn patience. The alternative is to do serious harm to the quality and standing of the judiciary, undermining an institution which, however imperfect, has been one of the more successful areas of English public life.

In its original form, this was delivered as the annual Bar Council Law Reform Lecture in November 2012. It reflected my experience over five years as a member of the Judicial Appointments Commission, the non-political body which since 2006 has been responsible for selecting those appointed to judicial office. Much has changed since it was delivered. The judiciary is a great deal more diverse than it was a decade ago. I have updated the text to reflect the current position. However, the judicial bench is still some way from full diversity, and the views expressed in 2012 remain relevant for the top courts as well as in other fields in which questions of diversity arise.

7

ABOLISHING PERSONAL
INJURIES LAW – A PROJECT

Personal injury litigation is big business. Accidental injury is common, allegations of negligence almost as common. Awards of damages can be high. Lawyers, claims handlers, experts and insurers are just some of the groups who thrive on this particular kind of human misfortune. The social cost is incalculable. What are we going to do about this, apart from taking better care of ourselves and others?

It is now more than twenty years since Patrick Atiyah published *The Damages Lottery*, one of the most eloquent polemics ever to be directed against a firmly entrenched principle of law. Professor Atiyah was concerned with the law of negligence generally. But his book has usually been treated as an attack on personal injuries law and its practitioners. Most of his arguments and all of his solutions were directed against the concept of fault-based liability for personal injury. He proposed to abolish liability in tort for causing personal injury. In the case of road accidents, then as now by far the largest single source of personal injury claims, the right to sue for negligence would be replaced by a system of compulsory, no-fault insurance against being injured. In the case of other sources of personal injury, there would be no alternative source of provision. Atiyah proposed to encourage people to buy insurance, but to leave it, in the final analysis, up to them.

Atiyah's criticisms had never previously been advanced with such rhetorical force. But they were not new. Many of them had appeared in his textbook *Accidents, Compensation and the Law*, the first edition of which appeared in 1970. A year before that, the Woodhouse Committee in New Zealand had proposed to replace the right to sue with a system of state-funded social provision. This recommendation was accepted by the New Zealand government and enacted in the Accident Compensation Act 1972. Even more radical proposals had been made by an Australian commission of inquiry, over which Sir Owen Woodhouse also presided, and of which Atiyah himself was a member. But these were never acted on. In England, the Pearson Commission had been appointed in 1973 and reported in 1978. It recommended a somewhat similar scheme, but funded from general taxation. After some years of hoping that the whole issue would go away, the British government eventually binned the report and resolved to take no action.

As a result, the issue had almost disappeared from sight by the time that *The Damages Lottery* was published in 1997. The book generated some brief ripples in the placid waters of academic journals. It is still read as a masterpiece of polemical contrarianism. But it completely failed in its main object, which was to interest the policymakers, journalists and general public to whom it was primarily addressed. Peter Cane's more recent editions of *Accidents, Compensation and the Law* have kept the cause alive. But his proposals, which are slightly different from Atiyah's, have had limited influence. You may well ask, then, why I should think it worth returning to this controversy now. There are at least two good reasons for doing so.

One is that we are witnessing a renewed bout of indignation about 'compensation culture'. This has been a recurring source of controversy in the press for some years, but more recently, the cause has been taken up by the government. In 2004 and again in 2012, government intervention followed intensive and very public lobbying by motor insurers. This resulted in a series of measures to curtail the activities of claims management companies, and changes to the solicitors' conduct rules. There have also been radical changes to the incidence of costs, most of which have been unfavourable to claimants. More recently, in 2018, the Civil Liability Act addressed the mounting cost of claims for whiplash injuries, many of which were believed to be unjustified or exaggerated. It required prescribed forms of medical evidence to be submitted before insurance claims for whiplash injuries could be settled, and introduced a statutory scale of damages awards. The mounting concern about compensation culture is powered by a number of factors. The main ones are the upward pressure on motor insurance premiums arising from an increase in the number and value of claims, governmental concern about the cost of claims against the National Health Service, and persistent stories in the press (not always accurate) about unmeritorious claims.

There is, however, a more fundamental reason for returning to Professor Atiyah's radical proposals. There are some propositions that are so deeply entrenched in the instincts of lawyers and the public at large that they are never critically examined. The duty of care to avoid causing physical injury to our fellows may well be the most deeply entrenched of all. As Lady Justice Hale observed in her judgment in the Court of Appeal in *Parkinson v St. James and Seacroft University Hospital NHS Trust* [2002] QB 266, at para 56, 'the right to bodily integrity is the first and most important of the interests protected by the law of tort'. By the leisurely standards of the common law, this is a relatively recent development. The modern law of negligence was made by nineteenth-century judges, who first recognised the existence of duties of care independent of the much older duties recognised by the law of trespass. This major development of our law occurred mainly in cases about negligently inflicted personal injury and property damage. The law of tort recognises these species of physical injury as inherently actionable. By comparison, purely economic interests are not generally actionable, but only in specific and carefully circumscribed cases. It is, as a general principle, desirable that judges and practitioners should reflect on the social and moral foundations of the law which they practise. The duty not negligently to injure other people is imposed by law, in other words by the state. Like any non-consensual obligation, it must ultimately be founded either on social utility or on collective moral values.

Atiyah's basic argument against the law of negligence was that it lacked social utility. Drawing mainly on the material collected by the Pearson Commission, he pointed out that almost all personal injury claims were brought against insured parties or public bodies. The Pearson Commission estimated that in 1973, 88 per cent of personal injury claims by number and 94 per cent by value were brought against insured parties, and most of the rest against public bodies. That conclusion will surprise no one. In most cases it is not worth suing anyone else. Given that most of the increase since Pearson comes from road accidents, where liability insurance is compulsory, the proportion of insured claims is likely to be at least as high today.

The cost of meeting claims for negligently caused personal injury was estimated by Pearson at about 1 per cent of the gross national product of the United Kingdom. There is a measure of uncertainty about all such estimates, but whatever the true proportion, it is a significant figure, and it represents a substantial social cost. In the first place, liabilities that fall to be met by insurers or by the state are effectively socialised across the population at large. We all, or almost all, pay for them in the form of higher insurance premiums or taxes. Studies suggest that although individual insurance premiums do to some extent vary with an individual's personal claims record, premiums are still largely fixed according to class of business and risk category.

Second, the cost is not limited to the amount of the damages. Perhaps the most remarkable figure in the statistical annexes to the Pearson Report was the committee's estimates of the cost of making and processing claims for personal injury. They concluded that legal and administrative costs amounted to 47 per cent of the total cost of settling personal injury claims. This figure was proposed subject to a large margin of error, but it is broadly consistent with other evidence. In 2017, the National Audit Office came up with a very similar figure, 45 per cent. There is no reason to think that the insurers' costs of processing claims against non-state bodies are any different.

Third, although the taxpayer has a bottomless pocket, insurers do not. Beyond a certain point, the cost of rising claims volumes cannot simply be piled on to premiums. They start to erode profits. Unless insurers make profits, they will not insure. The result will be a contraction of insurance capacity, followed by a scarcity that will sharply boost premiums. This is basic economics. In extreme cases, insurers can simply withdraw from the more exposed sectors of the liability market altogether. This is not a purely hypothetical prospect. It is what actually happened to product liability insurance in the United States in the late 1980s, as a direct result of the explosion of claims for long-term latent industrial diseases and environmental pollution. The market effectively ceased to exist, and had to be recreated offshore on more restrictive terms and at higher premiums.

A number of things might be thought to follow from the socialisation of the cost of personal injury claims. A system that makes compensation dependent on fault makes little sense if the damages are not being paid by the persons at fault, but by society as a whole. One is entitled to ask: why should the private law distribution of rights and liabilities between individuals or their employers determine the incidence of what is in reality a social cost? Let us leave the moral dimension out of it for the moment. I will return to it later. If the cost of compensating people for personal injury falls on society at large, there is no rational reason to distinguish between personal injury that has been caused by someone's fault, and personal injury that has occurred without fault. Equally, there is no rational reason why the victims of accidents, however caused, should necessarily recover a full indemnity as the law of tort presently requires. Since we are all paying for the tortiously inflicted injuries, we might as well treat it as a social service and make it respond to our collective social priorities rather than to the common-law rights of individual claimants.

Let me start with compensation culture. The problem about this protean phrase is that it is a slogan, and not a carefully thought-out position. It encompasses at least two complaints, which are very different although they share a common rhetoric. One is that too many fraudulent claims are being made: in other words people are being too greedy. The other is that too many justified claims are being made: in other words, the law is being too generous. The government seems to be making the first point, but Professor Atiyah was making the second.

There undoubtedly is a problem about fraudulent claims, but I do not think that it calls for a fundamental rethink of our law. Detected frauds have increased significantly, although how much of that is due to more diligent detection and how much to declining standards of honesty is hard to say. The main issue concerns small consumer claims, where it is likely to cost the insurers a great deal more to investigate a potentially fraudulent claim than just to pay up. Motor insurance fraud, which accounts for nearly two thirds of detected fraud, is particularly difficult for insurers to control through the terms of their contracts. Insurance is compulsory and contractual restrictions on cover or procedural conditions for payouts are tightly controlled by statute. So it may well be that legislation is needed in order to deal with it. But it is hard to regard this as raising a great issue of principle.

The more fundamental and controversial issue is not about fraudulent claims but about justified ones. There has been a persistent rise in both the number and value of claims for personal injuries. The Pearson Commission estimated that in 1973 there had been about 250,000 claims a year. According to the Association of British Insurers, the corresponding figure for 2013–14 was about 1.2 million. Since then, the number has been more or less stable, except in the exceptional period of the Covid-19 lockdown in 2020, when it saw a significant fall. Almost all of the increase since the 1970s was attributable to road accidents, which now account for about 80 per cent of all accidents. Since the number of road accidents does not seem to have increased in proportion, it is reasonable to conclude that the main factor at work is an increased propensity to claim, especially among those involved in road accidents. The Pearson Commission concluded that only 11 per cent of people injured in accidents even considered the possibility of claiming. Survey evidence suggested that by far the most significant reason was that they did not realise that they could. The main reason for that was ignorance: ignorance of the significance of their symptoms; ignorance of the law or the workings of the legal system; ignorance of the standards expected of others. It seems likely that the increased propensity to claim is due at least in part to greater knowledge of these matters. This is not in itself a bad thing. If people know more today about their rights, that may well be due, at least in part, to the active solicitation of claims by solicitors and claims management companies. To those like me who believe that litigation is an evil, the active solicitation of claims can seem distasteful. But it is really not a matter of taste, and I find it impossible to say that it is wrong. If the law entitles the victim of an accident to compensation, it ill becomes us to criticise the victim for knowing it and claiming. It is true, of course, that people who know that there is a claim to be made tend to reinterpret events in a way that justifies the claim. But there is nothing new about that, nor is it peculiar to personal injuries claims. Wish fulfilment is a basic trait of human nature, and a problem about witness evidence in every field of litigation.

Behind the growing propensity to claim lies another fundamental change which is perhaps even more significant. Unlike their forebears, people are no longer disposed to accept the wheel of fortune as an ordinary incident of human existence. They regard physical security not just as the normal state of affairs but as an entitlement. I do not find this surprising or discreditable. It is a perfectly rational response to some significant developments over the last half-century: higher expectations of government, to some extent encouraged by governments themselves; higher expectations of the law as an instrument of social welfare; higher professional standards; a more intense regulatory environment; and improvements in the technical competence of humanity, which have given us much more control over our own and other people's fortunes. The result of these developments is that a far higher proportion of personal injuries are regarded as avoidable. To say that injury was avoidable does not mean that it was negligently caused. But it is a major step in that direction. It has inevitably affected the standards of responsibility that the law imposes on us in our treatment of each other.

Judges have undoubtedly expanded the scope of duties of care over the past half-century, as well as the range of consequences for which a wrongdoer may be liable. But in doing this, they have merely followed the collective instincts and values of the public at large, which within limits is a legitimate influence on the common law. If the law says that we are entitled to blame other people for rather more of our misfortunes than hitherto, it is rather absurd to complain about a culture of blame, as if this was somehow a symptom of our collective moral degeneration. The importance of Professor Atiyah's work was that he was honest enough to recognise that if we want to influence the number and inci- dence of personal injury claims, the only way to do it is to alter people's legal rights, instead of going about lamenting the enforcement of what legal rights they have.

There are two basic criticisms to be made of the use of tort law to address the problems of personal injury, and they point in different directions. One is directed against the use of fault as the touchstone of liability. The other is directed at the scale of claims and at the corresponding social cost.

Let me deal with fault first. There are a number of argu- ments in favour of fault-free systems on the New Zealand model. One is that they are more efficient, because they avoid the considerable investigatory and legal costs of attrib- uting blame. The second is that if the object of the exercise is to address the problem of personal injury, there is no obvious reason to give special treatment to those victims who have had the good fortune to have been injured by someone else's fault. A third is that fault-based systems tend to influence behaviour in ways that are over-defensive and not necessarily in the public interest.

Let me take a well-known example, which illustrates all three points: the disputes in the latter half of the twentieth century about birth deformities attributed to drugs designed to relieve the symptoms of morning sickness in pregnancy. Thalidomide was invented in Germany. It was marketed as a treatment for nausea and insomnia in pregnancy, at a time when scientists believed that drugs taken by pregnant women could not cross the placental barrier and affect the developing foetus. This view was tragically mistaken, and as a result many thousands of babies were born with serious physical deformities. The drug was marketed in the UK between 1958 and 1961 by Distillers Biochemicals. The only cause of action available in England to the children who suffered the deformities was an action in tort against Distillers. This depended on proving negligence against Distillers, which formulated the product under licence but was neither the inventor nor the manufacturer of the active ingredient. It proved to be an expensive and time-consuming process with distinctly uncertain prospects of success. After six years of litigation there was a settlement in 1968 under which the allegations of negligence were withdrawn in return for an offer of 40 per cent of the proved damages. That even this much was achieved was due to a press campaign in which the main theme was that Distillers owed social and moral obligations going beyond the legal obligations imposed by the law of tort.

Now let me turn to another well-known case. Bendectin was the brand name of a product comprising vitamin B6 and a standard anti-histamine, which was marketed in the United States in the early 1980s for the treatment of morning sickness and insomnia in pregnancy. A number of women who had taken it gave birth to deformed babies. Yet these deformities were never shown to have been caused by Bendectin. Comprehensive testing both before and after the event showed it to be safe. It had been approved by the US Food and Drugs Administration, then one of the world's more effective drug licensing authorities, which had persistently refused to allow the marketing of thalidomide. Indeed, the FDA has recently reauthorised the marketing of the active ingredient of Bendectin under a different brand name. Yet the manufacturers had been forced to withdraw it from the market in 1983 because the cost of defending class actions made it unprofitable, even though none of these actions succeeded. Some of the literature suggests that the disappearance of Bendectin from the market for thirty years had serious consequences. It deterred drug companies from developing any drugs specifically designed for pregnant patients, and pushed many patients towards other less reputable and less intensively tested treatments.

The legal environment is very different in the United States, but defensive responses to the threat of liability are certainly not confined to America. *Tomlinson v Congleton Borough Council* [2004] 1 AC 46 is a good illustration of the way in which the fear of liability in tort can lead to the total withdrawal of facilities that are valued by the great majority of the population who use them responsibly. Mr Tomlinson dived head-first into a shallow lake at a well-known beauty spot and was paralysed for life. He sued the local authority for negligence. His case was that although the defendant put up warning notices, they knew that these were often ignored. They should therefore have protected him by putting the lake out of bounds and preventing the public from going there. The local authority ultimately did this, but only after the accident had occurred. The effect on the liberty of others was deplorable, and the House of Lords duly deplored it. But the reaction of the local authority was in fact a perfectly rational response to the problem posed by the current state of the law. Balancing risk of injury against the consequences of eliminating it requires a complex and no doubt expensive case-by-case assessment. From the point of view of the rational defendant, it is simpler, cheaper and safer to ban the

relevant activity, and far more likely to protect council officers from criticism when something goes wrong.

These are all in their different ways extreme cases. Nevertheless, they do show why the law of tort is an extraordinarily
clumsy and inefficient way of dealing with serious cases of
personal injury. It often misses the target, or hits the wrong
target. It makes us no safer, while producing undesirable side
effects. What is more, it does all of these things at disproportionate cost and with altogether excessive delay.

It is often suggested that fault is a necessary element in
any scheme of compensation, because it deters sloppy practices, thereby improving general standards of safety. I am
sceptical about this. Most of the available research has been
done in the United States. My tentative conclusion is that in
spite of the dramatically higher level of US damages awards,
it provides no convincing evidence of any deterrent effect
specifically attributable to the prospect of fault-based civil
liability. The whole notion of deterrence assumes that there
is a minimum of reflection behind the actor's decisions. Yet
negligence normally consists in the absence of reflection.
It generally happens through ignorance, incompetence or
oversight, none of them states of mind that are normally
associated with reflection upon the possible consequences.
On the roads, which is where the great majority of personal injuries occur, collisions are just as likely to injure the
negligent drivers themselves as other road-users. Yet for all
that, personal injuries sustained in road accidents have risen
inexorably.

The deterrence theory has more to be said for it at
the design stage. The designers of a safety procedure or a
product are deliberately applying their minds to the question
of safety. But even here, any deterrent effect is heavily diluted
by the availability of liability insurance, which is compulsory
in the case of liability to employees and normal in the case

of product liability to third parties. The evidence tends to suggest that the prospect of liability in tort achieves nothing that would not be achieved anyway by the prospect of reputational damage or criminal sanctions. Criminal sanctions are now more widely enacted and more efficiently enforced. They are also, as a general rule, uninsurable. All the survey evidence tends to suggest that as a way of educating those whose job it is to design for safety, such sanctions are a great deal more persuasive than the law of tort.

The law is generally sensitive to considerations of economic efficiency, although judges rarely acknowledge the fact. But one area which has been more or less impervious to considerations of economic efficiency is the legal right to bodily integrity. The debate about compensation culture really turns on complex cultural issues about moral responsibility and blame which have very little to do with economic efficiency. The public's view is based on two simple moral judgements. One is that the person who causes physical injury must make it good financially. The other is that it is a proper function of the courts to find facts and distribute blame, simply as a satisfaction for victims or their relatives. Questions of cost tend to seem trivial by comparison.

Personally, I would question whether there really is a moral case for imposing liability in damages on the ground of negligence. Negligence is not necessarily morally culpable. It is a normal feature of human behaviour. This is not the place to embark on a profound survey of corrective or distributive justice. I will only say this. I can imagine a moral case for imposing liability on those who cause physical damage to others, simply on the ground that they are the agents of some invasion of the victim's physical integrity. This implies strict liability. I can also imagine a moral case for imposing liability on those who intentionally or recklessly cause physical damage to others. But liability for negligence does not depend on a person's mere infliction of damage, nor on their state of mind. It depends on their falling below some objective standard of conduct to which they have not usually assented, but which the law imposes upon them. The only possible justification for the law doing that is its social utility. Yet the arbitrary results and incomplete coverage of a fault-based system, combined with its prodigious cost and unwelcome side effects, seriously undermine the social utility of the law of tort as a way of dealing with the problem.

To some extent, we are already moving towards a system of strict liability, or at any rate of stricter liability. This has been the tendency of legislation on the subject for some years. For example, strict liability is in principle imposed by the Animals Act for physical injury done by animals, and by the Consumer Protection Act for injury done by defective products offered for sale commercially. There are special defences in each case, but they are narrowly framed and even more narrowly applied. Such legislation seems to me to be a perfectly reasonable response to the general availability and widespread use of liability insurance in these classes of case. It would probably have made litigation such as that over thalidomide a great deal easier to resolve, had it been in force at the time. My own experience is that even in areas where traditional notions of fault prevail in theory, the courts have in practice moved closer to strict liability, albeit very gradually and without acknowledging that they are doing it. This is because the whole forensic process of attributing fault is inherently biased in favour of the claimant. Once it is established that something has gone wrong that was caused by the defendant's act, it can be very difficult to persuade a judge that it wasn't the defendant's fault. The court finds fault with all the forensic advantages of hindsight. The evidence will commonly reconstruct the exact chain of causation by which the injury occurred, starting from the injury and working backwards to the act. But the judge finding fault looks at the chain from the other end, starting with the defendant's act. The outcome seems obvious. What actually has happened was always going to happen. And what was always going to happen should have been obvious to the reasonable person, even if it wasn't at all obvious to the particular defendant. The forensic process lends a spurious clarity and inevitability to a chain of events that is actually a lot less straightforward. The result may be very like strict liability, but it is strict liability with most of the uncertainty and all of the costs associated with a fault-based system.

It will by now be apparent that I am not an admirer of our current system of distributing liability according to fault. But, and this is where the title of this essay is misleading, I have no doubt that it will survive. There are at least three reasons why it will survive. In the first place the only obvious alternative is a system of fault-free compensation funded either from taxation or by compulsory insurance. This would be a great deal less wasteful, because it would reduce the investigatory and legal costs of settling personal injury claims. But the enormous increase in the volume of claims which would occur if we dispensed with fault would enormously increase the overall cost. The New Zealand example is said to have been accepted by public opinion there, but it has not been adopted in any other common-law country. The second reason why fault will survive as the essential criterion for compensation is the phenomenon so familiar to economists of concentrated benefits but diffused costs. The hardships and costs associated with grave disabilities are visible and for those affected catastrophic; while the social costs of a fault-based system are subtle, indirect and thinly spread across the whole population. The one area where the public feels the cost directly is motor accidents. Annual motor premiums are a significant item in family budgets and we all notice when they go up. That no doubt accounts for the fact that government initiatives in this area have been concentrated in the motor sector. The third and perhaps most significant reason for its survival is that it responds to widespread public notions about personal responsibility and the proper function of law. I do not myself share these notions, but I am in a minority on this. It is fundamental to my conception of the judicial function that I do not sit just to give effect to my personal moral preferences.

My prediction is that fault will remain the touchstone of our law of personal injuries, but that the principle will be eroded at the edges by statutory intervention from one end and judicial hindsight from the other. The result will be to increase the overall cost of personal injury claims and, I suspect, to provoke a legislative reaction as mounting insurance premiums and pressures on the NHS budget lead to calls to control the costs. The outcome is likely to be the abolition of the principle of full indemnity and its replacement by a statutory measure of damages with a view to achieving a better balance between public and private interests. I would expect this to take two forms. One is the imposition of value thresholds on personal injury claims, with a view to eliminating small claims. Small claims account for the great majority of claims and are disproportionately costly and cumbersome to administer. The second will be the capping or abolition of certain heads of loss. There is a case for abolishing damages for non-pecuniary losses, or at least limiting it to long-term pain and suffering and loss of amenity. There is a case for limiting damages for loss of earnings to the amount necessary to support a reasonable standard of living, rather than the superior standard of living that the richest accident victims might have expected if they had not been injured.

To some extent these things are already happening. Successive decisions of the Supreme Court of Canada have limited the scope for large awards of non-pecuniary loss. The same trend is observable in the Judicial College guidelines in this country. In New South Wales, liability thresholds and caps on awards for loss of earnings were adopted for motor accidents by legislation enacted in 1999, and extended to other personal injury claims in 2002. The Civil Liability Act 2018 in the United Kingdom applies a rather similar system of thresholds and caps for whiplash injuries. It is I think significant, and indicative of the direction of travel, that the New South Wales legislation followed large and unpopular increases in insurance premiums. But it is also right to point out that it was accompanied by other measures making altogether more generous statutory provision for certain categories of victim than anything that has so far been contemplated in the United Kingdom. The statutory damages scheme for motor accidents extends in New South Wales to personal injuries occurring without fault. Moreover, since 2006 there has been a generous statutory scheme for compensating those suffering from personal injuries involving long-term care. Looking after the principal losers may be the price to be paid for limiting the generality of accident claims.

What all of this means is that the officers of this association can rest easy in their seats. It is likely to be needed for a considerable time to come.

This is an updated version of a lecture delivered to the Personal Injury Bar Association in November 2017.

8

A QUESTION OF TASTE: THE
SUPREME COURT AND THE
INTERPRETATION OF CONTRACTS

On 6 February 1663, Samuel Pepys recorded in his diary a meeting of the Tangier Committee. The committee was responsible for the administration of the port of Tangier in Morocco, one of England's earliest and most short-lived colonies. The business of the day was the drafting of a contract for the construction of a half-mile-long mole at the entrance to the harbour, one of the largest and most difficult civil engineering projects that the English government had undertaken for many decades. Ranged on one side of the table were the contractors: a naval officer, Sir John Lawson, and a courtier, Sir Hugh Cholmley. They were men of only passable honesty by the standards of the time. Lawson had at least been to Tangier, but he knew nothing about civil engineering. Cholmley claimed to be an expert on civil engineering on the strength of having built a jetty on his estate in Yorkshire, but he knew nothing about the port of Tangier. On the other side sat a group of senior officials of the Navy Board, none of whom knew anything about the construction of port facilities and most of whom knew nothing about Tangier either. Only one of them, the vice-admiral of England, had been there, and he had been bribed by the contractors. The parties set to drafting. A document was produced which in Pepys's opinion was completely incomprehensible, and after much discussion he gave it up as a waste of time and left. 'None of us that were there understood [it],' he wrote, 'but yet they agreed of things as Mr Cholmly and Sir J Lawson demanded, who are the undertakers; and so I left them to go on and agree, for I understood it not.'

Now, a modern contract lawyer, looking at this contract, would of course regard all of that as inadmissible and irrelevant. It is the founding principle of the law of contract that contracts are interpreted according to their objective meaning: the meaning that the words would have had to hypothetical reasonable people in their position, which may or may not coincide with the meaning that it had to the actual parties. The lawyer would start by examining the 'factual matrix', namely the information available to both sides and presumed to be known to them: the characteristics of the port of Tangier, the available techniques of construction, the properties of concrete and stone, and so forth. He would apply the ordinary presumption in building contracts that the contractors had informed themselves of the nature of the site and exigencies of performance. He would have assumed that the parties must have had in mind whatever disaster subsequently befell, and would impute to them some intention about what would happen in that event. He would diligently examine the language of the instrument as the parties should have understood it, comparing clause with clause to make a bargain that conformed to his own idea of commercial common sense. If necessary, he would manipulate the language to achieve a reasonable outcome. In other words, he would treat the parties as hypothetical abstractions rather than men of flesh and blood. He would put himself in their position, but with the benefit of a fair mind, the knowledge of a corps of expert geographers and engineers and no bribes, all characteristics that the actual participants

lacked. The moral of this story is that although in law sub-
jective opinion is no guide to the common intention of the
parties, objective construction may not be much better. Six
years after the contract was let, when the mole was still only
half built, the Navy Board lost patience, the contractors were
sacked and the contract cancelled. And serves them right,
says the contract lawyer. The incomplete works were shortly
afterwards washed away by a storm.

The interpretation of contracts can never be entirely free
of artifice. The main artifice, as I hope my little fable has
illustrated, is that the parties understood what they were
signing up to as completely as a judge armed with a mass of
objectively relevant and carefully analysed background information and the advantages of hindsight. One would think
that the language that the parties have agreed provided the
one sure foundation for a hypothetical reconstruction of
their intentions. However, rather more than thirty years ago,
the Judicial Committee of the House of Lords embarked
upon an ambitious attempt to free the interpretation of
contracts from the shackles of language and replace them
with some broader notion of intention. These attempts have
for the most part been associated with the towering figure
of Lord Hoffmann. More recently, however, the Supreme
Court has begun to withdraw from the more advanced positions seized during the Hoffmann offensive, to what I see as
a more defensible position. It is with these shifts of judicial
approach that I am now concerned.

The House of Lords' flight from language depended on
two closely related concepts. One was the 'surrounding circumstances'. The other was 'commercial common sense'.

The idea that the surrounding circumstances may be relevant to the meaning of language is commonly attributed to
that great judge Lord Wilberforce. He did not invent it. But
the most authoritative modern statements are due to him. In

two notable judgments,[2] Lord Wilberforce pointed out that when reading a contract the court must put itself in the position in which the parties stood at the time it was made, with all the knowledge that they had at the time about the origin and purpose of the transaction and the circumstances in which it would fall to be performed. But Lord Wilberforce's statement of this principle was deliberately restrained. He was not proposing to use the surrounding circumstances as an alternative way of discovering the parties' intentions. They were simply facts that assisted in interpreting the words. They helped one to know which, out of a range of plausible meanings, the parties must as reasonable people have had in mind.

However, a step change occurred with the decision of the House of Lords in *The Antaios* in 1984.[3] The dispute arose out of a three-year time-charter of a ship, which conferred a right of termination on the shipowner for non-payment of hire 'or on any breach of this charterparty'. One of the issues was whether this meant any breach, however minor, in which case it bore very harshly on the charterer; or only breaches sufficiently serious to deprive the shipowner of substantially the whole benefit of the contract, in which case it added nothing to the right of termination that he would have had anyway at common law. Having failed to persuade the arbitrators that it meant any breach at all, the shipowners applied for leave to appeal against the award. They were refused leave in the High Court, and again in the Court of Appeal and the House of Lords, mainly on the grounds that their appeal had no merit. The problem about the case lies not with the result, which seems fair enough, but with the extravagant language in which it was justified by Lord Diplock. He famously declared that 'if detailed semantic and syntactical analysis of words in a commercial contract is going to lead to a conclusion that flouts business common sense, it must be made to yield to business common sense'. On the face of it, Lord Diplock was commending the use of commercial common sense not as a means of understanding the language of the contract, but as a means of overriding it. As a rule of interpretation, this seems both unnecessary and wrong. Yet it is one of the few parts of the law reports that most commercial judges can quote from memory. It is cited to them in virtually every case where counsel contends for a result that is inconsistent with what his client appears to have agreed.

Commenting on the decision two decades later, Lord Steyn observed that it was part of a 'shift from literal methods of interpretation to a more commercial approach'.[4] As an example of the literalism which we had now put behind us, Lord Steyn cited from Paley's *Moral and Political Philosophy* the story of the tyrant Temures. Temures was the general who promised the garrison of Sebastia that if they surrendered no blood would be shed. When they surrendered, he had them buried alive. This delightful little anecdote was actually cited by Paley as an example of using the literal as opposed to the colloquial meaning of words. To most people, 'shedding blood' simply meant killing. As a description of the approach to construction adopted by the English courts before *The Antaios*, the story is a travesty. The common law has never, since the modern law of contract was developed in the nineteenth century, adopted literalism as a rule of interpretation. It has always recognised that language is imprecise, that context may modify its meaning, and that words may be used in a special sense. In England, Baron Parke observed as early as 1848 that 'greater regard is to be had to the clear intent of the parties than to any particular words which they may have used in the expression of their intent'.[5] The older cases are full of warnings against the dangers posed by a wooden adherence to the disembodied meaning of words.

The real distinction is not between a literal and a commercial interpretation. It is between an approach to contractual interpretation that elucidates the meaning of the words, and an approach that modifies or contradicts the words in pursuit of what appears to a judge to be a reasonable result.

For some years, Lord Diplock's pronouncement was not taken at face value. Although frequently cited, it was regarded as a mere expletive. But at the end of the last century, the mood changed. It was a period when traditional views about the interpretation of all written instruments were under challenge, not just contracts but patents, deeds and statutes. As far as contracts were concerned, an early sign of the direction of travel was the decision of the House of Lords in *Charter Reinsurance Co. v Fagan*.[6] This was a dispute about a programme of whole account excess of loss reinsurance. The reinsurer's liability kicked in once the reinsured's losses exceeded an ultimate net loss of a given amount. The definition of an ultimate net loss depended on what the reinsured had 'actually paid' in settlement of claims. The reinsured went into liquidation and consequently he actually paid very little. But the Court of Appeal and the House of Lords held that the words 'actually paid' did not mean that the reinsured had to have ... well ... actually paid. It was enough that the reinsured was liable to pay it although he had not done so and in view of his insolvency probably never would. We have truly reached the ultimate point which the flexibility of language can attain, when we find that in a court of law, language means precisely the opposite of what it says.

As it happens, although I was the unsuccessful counsel in that case, I think that the decision was right. It was right essentially for the reasons given by Lord Mustill. He based his analysis on the technical meaning given to the concept of payment in the world of insurance and in the case law extending back for more than a century. Lord Hoffmann, however, proposed a more radical solution. His line was that language is such a flexible instrument that words commonly have no 'ordinary and natural meaning'. They have a variety of meanings depending on the context. He illustrated the point with a homely example. A wife comes home with a new dress and the husband asks how much she paid for it.

> 'She would not be understanding his question in its natural meaning,' said Lord Hoffmann if she answered: 'Nothing, because the shop gave me 30 days' credit.' It is perfectly clear from the context that the husband wanted to know the amount of the liability which she incurred, whether or not that liability has been discharged.'

What is true, he concludes, of ordinary speech is also true of reinsurance. This argument is the direct opposite of Lord Mustill's. Where Lord Mustill had emphasised the technical meaning of insurance terminology, Lord Hoffmann based his view on the inherent adaptability of all language. Lord Mustill used a special dictionary where Lord Hoffmann threw the dictionary away. The problem about his homely example of the wife's new dress is, of course, that the context that he is imagining is one where we cannot reasonably expect language to be used exactly. In this respect it is quite unlike the context with which I am concerned now, with two parties making a binding contract at arms' length. Moreover, exchanges between husband and wife are not generally subject to the rule of objective construction. Either of them can ask the one question which the court is not allowed to ask, namely 'What do you mean?'.

Lord Mustill expressed his reservations about this approach in his own judgment, in terms which appear to me to have considerable force.

I believe [he said] that most expressions do have a natural meaning, in the sense of their primary meaning in ordinary speech. Certainly, there are occasions where direct recourse to such a meaning is inappropriate. Thus, the word may come from a specialist vocabulary and have no significance in ordinary speech. Or it may have one meaning in common speech and another in a specialist vocabulary; and the content may show that the author of the document in which it appears intended it to be understood in the latter sense. Subject to this, however, the inquiry will start, and usually finish, by asking what is the ordinary meaning of the words used.

Nonetheless, it took only a year for Lord Hoffmann's approach to prevail. The moment came in 1998 in one of the most influential modern decisions on the construction of interpretation, *Investors Compensation Scheme Ltd v West Bromwich Building Society*,[7] in which Lord Hoffmann delivered the leading speech. It has more than once been suggested that this famous judgment was only a restatement of principles which were already familiar and uncontroversial. It is true that what is radical about it is perhaps more its tone than its substance. But instinct and mood play an important role in judicial analysis, and *ICS* changed the mood among judges dealing with commercial contracts in ways that are altogether more fundamental. I am not going to suggest that Lord Hoffmann has been misunderstood. I think that that is exactly what he intended to do.

In his speech, he began by observing that 'all the old baggage of "legal" interpretation' had been discarded. Having thus laid to one side the considered analyses of generations of careful contract lawyers, Lord Hoffmann formulated five principles which he suggested had replaced them. The first three principles are mainly concerned to broaden the range of facts which could serve as relevant surrounding circumstances, so as to include 'absolutely anything' that would have affected the way in which the contract would have been understood by a reasonable man apart from pre-contractual negotiations and information unavailable to the parties. But the most striking of his five principles were the fourth and fifth. The fourth principle was founded on a distinction between language and meaning. Language, he suggested, was a mere matter of dictionaries and grammar. Meaning was something different, namely what the document would convey to a reasonable person against the relevant background. The background, he said, 'may not merely enable the reasonable man to choose between the possible meanings of words which are ambiguous but even (as occasionally happens in ordinary life) to conclude that the parties must, for whatever reason, have used the wrong words or syntax'.

In other words, the background may not only enable one to choose between possible meanings of the words, but to select impossible ones instead. The fifth principle builds upon that proposition. It was that the traditional adoption of the 'natural and ordinary meaning' of language is no more than a rebuttable presumption that people mean what they say in formal documents. If the background suggests that something has gone wrong with the words, the law may attribute a different intention to them. In support of this, he cited Lord Diplock's famous observation in *The Antaios*.

What did Lord Hoffmann mean by suggesting that something might have gone wrong with the words? He clearly did not have in mind a case where the text just became garbled in the word processor or the verb had been accidentally omitted. Looking through his seductive prose, what he actually appears to have meant is that the background may be used to show that the parties cannot as reasonable people have meant what they said, so that the court is entitled to substitute something else. Lord Hoffmann does not spell out how we are to discover what else they meant if it was not what they said. But the only plausible answer to that question is that the parties are taken to have intended whatever reasonable people would have intended, even if it is not a possible meaning of the words. The subsequent case law demonstrates very clearly where this leads. It commonly involves treating the background circumstances as an alternative guide to the parties' intentions instead of a means of interpreting their language.

Chartbrook Ltd v Persimmon Homes Ltd[8] was an appeal to the House of Lords which turned on the interpretation of a contract between a landowner and a developer. The relevant clauses determined the amount to be paid to the landowner on the successful completion and sale of the plots. The landowner claimed to be entitled to about five times what the developer thought was due. The developer's case was based on the express terms of the agreement, in particular the definition clauses in which the parties described what they meant by the terms used. But the House of Lords held that something had gone wrong with the language. It is true that it was not garbled. The sentences used intelligible words. There were subjects, verbs and objects. There was no apparent error of drafting. But Lord Hoffmann reconstructed the commercial logic of the transaction on the assumption that it was highly unlikely that land values would fall. From this, he concluded that on the developer's construction the result was more favourable to him than the parties can have intended. The result may well have been just, but I have some difficulty in recognising in it a process of interpretation. Moreover, if the case had been decided two decades earlier, when property values were indeed falling fast, it may be that Lord Hoffmann's view about the parties expectations would have been different.

A further stage was reached with the decision in *Rainy Sky v Kookmin Bank* in 2011.[9] The dispute in this case was about the scope of a bank guarantee given in connection with a shipbuilding contract. The guarantee covered the repayment of certain advance instalments of the price in the event that the ship was not delivered. But there was a dispute about which kinds of advance instalments were covered. The bank contended that not all of the advances were covered. The language on the face of it supported its view. The Court of Appeal accepted this. Their reason was that although there was no obvious commercial reason why the buyers should have been prepared to accept less than a full guarantee of the advance instalments, this result was neither absurd nor irrational and on the face of the contract that is what they had agreed. Lord Justice Patten, delivering the leading judgment for the majority in the Court of Appeal, observed that on any other view they were 'in real danger of substituting our own judgment of the commerciality of the transaction for that of those who were actually party to it' (para 51). The Supreme Court reversed them on the ground that it was not necessary to show that the apparent meaning of the contract was absurd or irrational. It was enough that there was no plausible reason why the guarantee should have been for less than the full amount of the advances. Lord Clarke, in his leading judgment, emphasised that the object was to understand rather than override the language. But his reasoning points the other way. In the absence of an explanation, the court thought it objectively more reasonable that there should be a full guarantee than a partial one. It followed that the words which pointed to a partial one did not really represent the parties' intentions.

I suspect that some, perhaps most, of these cases might have been decided in the same way on more traditional principles of interpretation. But there are, I would suggest, a number of problems about the approach to construction that they adopted.

The first and main point to make is that the language of the parties' agreement, read as a whole, is the only direct evidence of their intentions which is admissible in a court of law. I would certainly not advocate literalism as an approach to construction. But it is a fallacy to say that language is meaningful only in relation to some particular background. Most language and all properly drafted language has an autonomous meaning. I find the belittling of dictionaries and grammars as tools of interpretation to be rather extraordinary. Language is a mode of communication. Its efficacy depends on the acceptance of a number of conventions that enable people to understand each other. Dictionaries and grammars are simply reference books that record these conventions. If we abandon them as the basic tools of construction, we are no longer discovering how the parties understood each other. We are simply leaving judges to reconstruct an ideal contract which the parties might have been wiser to make, but never did.

I think that it is time to reassert the primacy of language in the interpretation of contracts. It is true that language is a flexible instrument. But let us not overstate its flexibility. Language, properly used, should speak for itself and it usually does. The more precise the words used and the more elaborate the drafting, the less likely it is that the surrounding circumstances will add anything useful. I do not therefore accept that the flexibility of language is a proper basis for treating the surrounding circumstances as an independent source from which to discover the parties' objective intentions. The surrounding circumstances may well enable us to discover what the objective was, but not how far it has been achieved. In a negotiation, the parties' objectives are likely to be different. In the *Rainy Sky*, for example, it was in the interest of the purchaser to get as much as it could out of the guarantor bank. The surrounding circumstances cannot tell us how far he succeeded in that endeavour, as against a bank whose interest was to concede as little as possible. Only the language can tell us that. The parties have no way to tell the court what they really want other than by deploying words. They are the masters of their own agreement, and anything that marginalises the role of their words in the process of construction is a direct assault on their autonomy.

That brings me to the second major problem about the use of the surrounding circumstances to modify the effect of language. This is the difficulty of applying it fairly in a legal system like ours which rigorously excludes the use of pre-contractual negotiations as evidence of intention. In *Investors Compensation Scheme*, Lord Hoffmann described the exclusion of pre-contractual negotiations as being based on 'reasons of practical policy'. But the reason is actually more fundamental than that. The exclusionary rule follows from the objective character of all contractual interpretation. The course of the negotiations cannot tell us what the contract objectively meant. It can tell us only what one or other or both of the parties subjectively thought or assumed or hoped that it meant. But if we cannot resort to the parties' thoughts, assumptions or hopes, how are we to answer the question posed by Lord Clarke in the *Rainy Sky*. The main reason that he gave for adopting the purchaser's construction of the guarantee was that no plausible commercial explanation had been given for why the guarantee should cover less than the whole amount of the prepayments. It is not normally the function of a contract to explain why it is in the terms that it is. Lord Clarke's question can be answered only by reference to the views of the parties. Yet that is the one source of information that is barred by law. An apparently harsh or unreasonable term may have been agreed by way of compromise or in exchange for concessions in other areas or because the deal was concluded at 3 a.m. and one of the parties was more interested in going to bed than in the finer points of drafting. It seems extraordinarily unfair to the guarantor bank that it should have been prevented by law from answering the question that turned out to be decisive of the issue of construction, namely 'Why did you agree this?' Once the courts resort to sources other than the language in order to identify the object of the transaction, it is difficult to justify the current rule which excludes extrinsic evidence. Yet that rule is fundamental to the principle of objective construction and has been reaffirmed in almost every case where the *Investors Compensation Scheme* approach has been applied.

My third difficulty with the *Investors Compensation Scheme* approach is that judges are not necessarily well placed to decide what commercial common sense requires. Judges start from the answer and work backwards. They come to the question of interpretation after the dispute has arisen, when the parties are at loggerheads. They understandably focus on what has gone wrong, and look to the contract to put it right. Their instincts about what the parties must have intended are therefore likely to be quite different from that of the parties themselves at the time that the contract was originally agreed, when they did not have the eventual catastrophe in mind. Moreover, judges' notions of common sense tend to be moulded by their idea of fairness. But fairness has nothing to do with commercial contracts. The parties enter into them in a spirit of competitive cooperation, with a view to serving their own interests. Those interests are likely to conflict. Commercial parties can be most unfair and entirely unreasonable, if they can get away with it. The problem about measuring their intentions by a yardstick of commercial common sense is that in practice it transforms the judge from an interpreter into a kind of *amiable compositeur*. It becomes a means of saving one party from what has turned out to be a bad bargain. The question is no longer what the parties agreed. It is what would they have agreed if they were the objective, just and fair-minded people that in practice they hardly ever are.

Every practitioner will have his own illustrations drawn from his own experience. For my part I will mention just one example which frequently struck me when I was in practice. Long-term contracts commonly include clauses giving one party an option to terminate in certain events, for example if a given standard of performance is not achieved, or not achieved by a given date. In my experience, commercial parties attach importance to such clauses. They may want to deter non-performance. They frequently want a let-out if the situation changes in a way that may adversely affect them. But commercial judges in England are traditionally hostile to peremptory termination clauses. The problem about them is that they are rarely invoked for the reasons for which they were originally included. A party with a right to terminate will only do it if it suits their broader commercial interest. Time-chartered ships are never withdrawn by the shipowners for non-payment of hire if the market has gone down since it was agreed. If they were, the shipowner would get less money from the replacement charter. Time-chartered ships are only withdrawn if there is a chance to recharter them at a higher rate, perhaps to the same charterer. To a judge looking for the fair result after the termination right has been exercised (or purportedly exercised) this seems unfair. It smacks of bad faith. So they tend to interpret the clauses more narrowly than the parties envisaged when they agreed it. This is just one illustration of the broader truth that judicial and commercial attitudes overlap but do not coincide.

Finally, the broader approach to construction favoured by

Lord Hoffmann is difficult to reconcile with the law relating to implied terms and rectification. It is hard to see any need for either of these legal concepts if the parties can have an intention attributed to them that is not reflected in the language of the agreement.

In *Attorney-General of Belize v Belize Telecom Ltd*,[10] Lord Hoffmann, delivering the advice of the Privy Council, came close to abolishing the implication of terms as a distinct legal concept, at any rate in cases where the implication was said to arise from the particular facts rather than from any general principle of law. It was all, he said, a question of interpretation. But this, with respect, cannot possibly be right. The point about an implied term is that the parties have not expressed it. Implication fills a gap in the written instrument. It is not possible to identify by a process of interpretation something that *ex hypothesi* is not in the agreement at all. The minimum condition for the recognition of an implied term is that it must be necessary in order to prevent the contract from being futile, ineffective or absurd. The problem about the process of interpretation described by Lord Hoffmann in *Investors Compensation Scheme* is that it is in reality a process of implication but without reference to the concept of necessity. When combined with his analysis in *Belize*, it is tantamount to allowing terms to be implied on the grounds that they are commercially reasonable and must therefore have been intended. This solution has had its advocates. It was famously favoured by Lord Denning. But it was decisively rejected by the House of Lords in *Liverpool City Council v Irwin*. It may be, as the Supreme Court has recently suggested, that Lord Hoffmann has been misunderstood, but I doubt it. Lord Hoffmann was not a judge who decided things by accident. At any rate, it seems clear from the recent and unanimous decision of the Supreme Court in *Marks & Spencer Plc v BNP Paribas Securities Services Trust Co*,[11] that the traditional distinction between construction and implication still exists.

Very similar problems arise in relation to the law of rectification. A contract may be rectified if the terms fail correctly to express the parties' true agreement. Where it is obvious that a word has been omitted and what the word is, the courts have long recognised that it may be reinserted as a matter of interpretation without going to the length of applying for rectification. But this is an exacting test. By comparison, the issue cannot arise at all if Lord Hoffmann was right in *Investors Compensation Scheme*. His view was that where something has gone wrong with the words, the correct response is to divine what the parties meant from the surrounding circumstances or the underlying commercial objective. This is a real problem, not just a point of form or a question of labels. The law about rectification is based on the proposition that the parties must be taken to have meant what they said, a proposition which is reduced by Lord Hoffmann to the status of a rebuttable presumption. For that reason, the legal criteria for rectifying a contract are extremely exacting. Once those criteria are satisfied, evidence that would not be admissible for the purpose of interpreting the document becomes admissible for the purpose of rectifying it. That will include evidence of pre-contractual negotiations. This is a radically different process, which is largely circumvented by the approach that Lord Hoffmann has taken to questions of implication.

These considerations provide some at least of the reasons why the Supreme Court has recently sounded the retreat. In the recent case of *Arnold v Britton*[12] the Supreme Court had to consider a contract for the sale of leasehold property on a newly developed estate. The contract provided for the payment of service charges. These were to be calculated by reference to an escalation clause that might just about have made sense in the economic conditions of the 1970s, when it was agreed, but produced a grotesque result once those conditions changed. Lord Neuberger, delivering the leading judgment, set out a number of principles that reasserted some traditional orthodoxies from earlier case law. These included the primacy of language in the interpretation of contracts. He also pointed out the danger of retrospectively applying a notion of commercial common sense influenced by what had gone wrong after the contract was made. But if the Supreme Court has sounded the retreat, it has, I must admit, sounded it in rather muffled tones. It has not actually admitted that earlier decisions went too far. The decisions in *Investors Compensation Scheme* or *Rainy Sky* have not been overruled.[13]

It is not entirely clear how the Supreme Court will ultimately resolve these differences. But some indication of the new direction of travel can be seen from the recent judgment of a unanimous court in *Wood v Capita Insurance Services*.[14] This case was about a contract for the sale of an insurance company. The contract contained a provision entitling the buyer of the business to be indemnified against compensation payable to customers for certain mis-selling claims arising out of the conduct of the business by the old management. The words made an apparently arbitrary distinction between cases where customers complained and cases where the company was forced to compensate them by regulators. In the High Court, the judge held that although the indemnity appeared to extend only to cases where the customer had complained, it must have been intended to apply in either case. The Court of Appeal disagreed and gave effect to the words of the clause. The Supreme Court upheld the Court of Appeal. The reality was that the buyers had an interest in getting the broadest possible indemnity, and the sellers had an equal and opposite interest in conceding the narrowest possible one. As Lord Hodge, delivering the leading judgment, observed,

> Business common sense is useful to ascertain the purpose of a provision and how it might operate in practice. But in the tug o' war of commercial negotiation, business common sense can rarely assist the court in ascertaining on which side of the line the centre line marking on the tug o' war rope lay, when the negotiations ended.

He therefore applied the language of the contract, which favoured the sellers. It was a harsh result, but there were reasons apparent from other provisions of the contract why the parties could rationally have intended it.

Just as *ICS* changed the judicial mood about language and tended to encourage the view that it was basically unimportant, so the more recent cases may in due course be seen to have changed it back again, at least to some degree. Experience has suggested that the loose approach to the construction of commercial documents which reached its highest point in *Rainy Sky* may have done a disservice to commercial parties by depriving them of the only effective means of making their intentions known.

The late Lord Diplock was a man who liked to be right, even by the self-confident standard of Her Majesty's judges. He once wrote a speech in an appeal on a question of contractual interpretation, in which he said that although he thought that his colleagues were wrong he proposed to agree with them. This, he said, was because the House of Lords was the final court of appeal. It followed that a contract must mean whatever at least three out of five law lords said it meant.[15] As a rule of interpretation, this seems less than helpful. I hope that in future we can do better than that.

This essay was originally delivered as the Harris Society Annual Lecture at Keble College, Oxford, in May 2017. I have made minor changes designed to explain legal terms or concepts for a non-legal reader.

THE CONSTITUTION: TOWARDS
AN UNCERTAIN FUTURE

9

BREXIT: A PRIMER FOR FOREIGNERS

I sat for seven years on the Supreme Court of the United Kingdom. The Supreme Court hears appeals which are thought to have important implications for the development of the law. They include cases about land law, contract law, tort law and so on. But over the last few years, the Supreme Court has assumed an increasingly prominent constitutional role. This has been due mainly to the passions aroused in the United Kingdom by the referendum of 2016, which resulted in a majority vote to leave the European Union. The decision provoked a major political crisis, the most serious in Britain since the 1930s. It divided our society. It put great pressure on our constitution and on many of our institutions, notably Parliament, the civil service and the major political parties. A decision of such fundamental importance calls for explanation, especially when the factors at work are complicated and far from obvious.

The British decision to leave the European Union is widely misunderstood in continental Europe. I have developed many strange habits over the years, and one of them is to read the international press. I read the French and German press most days, and sometimes the Italian and Spanish press as well. Press coverage of Brexit is better in Germany than, for example, in France. Nevertheless, anyone regularly reading the press in either country would get the impression that the British are at best naïve and at worst mad. There are three standard explanations that one encounters time after time. One – the British are gripped by post-imperial nostalgia and delusions of grandeur. Two – the British have succumbed to racism and xenophobia. Three – the British do not know what they are doing because they have been deceived by lying politicians. If you look hard enough, you can find examples in Britain's recent history to support all of these explanations. But they are all superficial and misleading. Personally, I disagree with the decision that most of my fellow countrymen made in 2016. I think that they have made a serious mistake that will do lasting damage to our economy. But they are not mad. They are not irrational, not naïve, and have not been deceived. Some of their reasons are specific to the United Kingdom, but some of them are relevant to the whole of the European Union, and hold lessons which it would be foolish for the rest of Europe to ignore.

Let me first address the suggestion that we have been gripped by racism and xenophobia. There are, I regret to say, racists and xenophobes in Britain, just as there are in other European countries. But we should not overstate either their numbers or their influence. There have been a very small number of incidents of verbal abuse of migrants, which have provoked universal disapproval. We have had no racially motivated riots. Accusations of racism and xenophobia have tended to revolve around British attitudes to immigration. Britain has for some years been a high-wage economy with low levels of unemployment. It has a highly flexible labour market. It chose not to restrict migration from new European Union members in eastern Europe during the transitional period after they joined. These factors, in addition to widespread use of English as a second language, have inevitably made Britain an attractive destination for migrants from both inside and outside the European Union. Over the past decade we have had the highest level of immigration in

Europe after Germany. One does not have to resort to racism or xenophobia to explain why this has caused difficulty. In a high employment economy, there is no plausible case for saying that migrants take other people's jobs, although they may limit wage growth. The real concerns have been about the identity of traditional communities, and about increased pressure on housing and other public services such as education and health. But the link between concerns like these and Brexit is rather remote. For obvious reasons, historic immigration has generally been concentrated in the more prosperous regions of Britain, in particular London. Yet the more prosperous regions have absorbed the immigrants without much difficulty, and those regions voted to stay in the European Union. The areas that registered the highest leave votes in the referendum tended to have relatively low levels of immigration.

During the referendum campaign of 2016, immigration was certainly an issue, but that was because of fears for the future rather than historic experience. The timing of the referendum was unfortunate. The campaign was fought in the midst of the controversy provoked by the German government's decision to admit very large numbers of refugees from the Middle and Near East. News pictures of hundreds of thousands of refugees hammering at the gates of eastern Europe, followed by reports of the attempts of the German government to redistribute some of them to other EU countries, made a powerful impression in Britain. Since the 2016 referendum, concern about immigration has sharply declined, partly because the National Health Service, the care sector, and much of the service sector of the economy have been shown to depend heavily on imported labour. A telling sign of this was that Mr Farage's party, originally UKIP and then the Brexit Party, which beat the drum loudest on immigration in 2016, virtually abandoned the issue during the election campaigns of 2019. Immigration had lost its capacity to influence voters.

Next, there is the familiar trope about the British being locked in a time warp, dominated by wartime triumphs and fantasies of imperial greatness. Of course, historical experience is an important part of any society's identity, even among those who have only the haziest idea of their history. The fact that Britain was the only European country (apart from Sweden and Switzerland) to escape totalitarianism or foreign occupation in the 1930s and 1940s explains much about the attitudes of British statesmen of the immediate post-war period to Europe. But today the impact of Britain's imperial and wartime past is very slight. Our experience of decolonisation was relatively benign. We did not fight debilitating wars to suppress independence movements in our colonies. We were not brought to the edge of civil war, as France was. Indian independence in 1947 was marred in India itself by the intercommunal strife provoked by the partition of the subcontinent into two states. But it provoked very little controversy in Britain. The rapid decolonisation of the 1960s was a bipartisan process, to which no one took exception in Britain apart from a marginal group of right-wing Tory politicians gathered round the then Earl of Salisbury. It is doubtful whether the British working classes were ever much interested in the empire. It appealed mainly to middle-class people, to whom it offered a career with a status that few of them could have achieved in Britain. But they have long ago moved on. If there was any part of the United Kingdom where one would have expected to find post-imperial nostalgia it was Scotland. The Scots played a part in the acquisition and government of the British Empire that was out of all proportion to their numbers. They provided a large proportion of the soldiers, administrators and settlers. The empire had a higher profile in Scotland than it did in any other part of the United Kingdom. Yet in the referendum Scotland produced a larger vote for remaining in the EU than any other region. I think that we can forget this particular cliché of post-referendum analysis.

Let me now turn to the suggestion that the British were deceived by lying politicians. Lies, exaggerations and wishful thinking are unfortunately a routine feature of electioneering in all countries, and Britain is no exception. There were plenty of lies told in the referendum campaign of 2016, most of them by the Leave side. The most notorious one was the statement on the side of the Leave campaign's bus that Britain paid £350 million a week to the European Union that could otherwise be spent on the National Health Service. But voters are smart and most of them are quite well informed. They do not believe everything that politicians tell them. Newspapers have noticeable biases, but radio and television, which are most people's main source of news and information on current affairs, are politically neutral and highly informative. The lie on the side of the Leave campaign's bus was comprehensively exposed during the campaign, and I do not think that many people believed it. Anyway, it would have made no difference. The true figure was large enough. Britain is the biggest net contributor to the European Union budget after Germany.

Most of the misleading statements made during the referendum campaign were not really lies. They were forecasts of the economic consequences of leaving the European Union which were inevitably speculative, and often grossly exaggerated. The Leave campaign argued that it would be easy to negotiate a deal with the European Union that would give us the benefits of membership without the burdens, and that we could do better trade deals with the rest of the world with 65 million consumers than the European Union could with 450 million. These arguments were absurd. But the Remain campaign's pessimistic predictions of disaster if we left were also seriously exaggerated. We may be poorer outside the European Union, depending on the terms of any trade agreement that we make with them. Sensible people should regret that, but it will not be catastrophic. The real problem was not the lies. It was the fact that people had to vote on a question the implications of which depended on negotiations with the European Union and could not be known in advance.

The clearest evidence that the British were not deceived is that although the economic difficulties of Brexit have become increasingly obvious, opinion about the European Union has hardly shifted since the referendum. This is reflected in the opinion polls published at regular intervals since 2016. Some people who voted to leave have become remainers as a result of the mounting evidence of economic difficulty ahead. Others who voted to remain, like Jeremy Hunt, the foreign secretary in 2018 and 2019, became leavers because they were repelled by what they saw as the inflexibility and arrogance with which the negotiations were handled by the European Union. Frankly, people got fed up with the tendentious leaks emanating from the commission and the schoolmasterly lectures of Michel Barnier. I regret to say that every public statement made by the European Parliament's Brexit coordinator Mr Verhofstad probably added many thousand votes to the Leave side of the argument. I would not for a moment seek to defend the way that my government handled the negotiations. They never sat down to work out what the European Union could afford to concede. Mrs May, who never had a secure parliamentary majority, committed herself at an early stage to negotiating objectives that were unachievable. They were directed mainly at satisfying the extremists in her own party on whose votes she depended. But those who believed in membership of the European Union were constantly dismayed by the undiplomatic and rigid behaviour of the European Union. At a crucial time when opinion in Britain might have shifted in favour of the European Union, the public statements of prominent European Union politicians showed the union's most unattractive side.

The current state of British public opinion can be measured by the outcome of the general election of December 2019. The most that remainers could ever sensibly have hoped for was a second referendum, fought on the basis of the much fuller information that had become available since 2016. They believed that it might produce a different decision. But it is now clear that the result of a second referendum would probably have been the same as the first, and by a larger margin. Brexit was the dominant issue in the general election. The Tory party, which was the only party to reject a second referendum, obtained the largest majority it has achieved in thirty years. The Labour Party's support for a second referendum cost it many seats in the Midlands and the north of England which had never elected a Tory Member of Parliament since democracy began. The Liberal Democrats, who campaigned on a policy of revoking Brexit, got nowhere and its leader lost her seat. A number of Members of Parliament had left the Tory party in protest against its anti-European programme and stood in their old constituencies as independents. They included politicians of real public stature who had been ministers in Tory governments and had represented their constituencies for many years, such as Dominic Grieve and David Gauke. Every one of them was defeated by a large majority, usually by novice politicians whom no one had previously heard of, but who subscribed to the Tory party's Brexit programme.

Two conclusions inescapably emerge.

The first is that Britain is leaving the European Union with its eyes open. The British knew what they were doing. They have not been engaged in some delusionary protest against globalisation or the domestic economic policies of the last government. They are not living in a make-believe world like those who voted for Trump in the United States. All of these patronising explanations of their decision seem to me to be mere attempts to evade unpalatable truths. The British voted to leave the European Union because they wanted to leave the European Union.

The second conclusion is that economic considerations, although obviously relevant, have not been decisive. By 2019, the British were well aware of the economic risks of leaving the European Union. They naturally hoped that those risks could be mitigated by agreement. But a majority wish to leave anyway. It is a striking fact that the regions that have produced the largest majorities for leaving the European Union were often those that receive the largest economic benefits from membership. Regions such as Wales, Cornwall and Humberside were big recipients of European Union structural funds but clocked up some of the largest majorities for leaving. Regions in the northeast, like Sunderland, have major manufacturing plants, notably in the car industry, which were heavily dependent on trading links with the European Union. They too voted to leave. Agricultural communities have benefited handsomely from the common agricultural policy for decades. Most of them voted to leave. The scale of the Tory victory and its regional distribution show that there is now a substantial majority who are irretrievably hostile to membership of the European Union, for reasons that are essentially political and not economic.

What might those political reasons be? They are summed up in the words 'Take back control', which was the slogan of the Leave campaign during the 2016 referendum. The basic problem about British attitudes to the European Union has been that the British never accepted the political dimension of the European project. They always regarded it as an arrangement for mutual economic advantage, and nothing more. The British accept that there are economic concessions, sometimes large economic concessions, that have to be made in order to obtain economic access to other peoples' markets. But they have never been happy to concede their sovereignty as a nation to a supranational political order. The embodiment of Britain's traditional view of its national sovereignty is a Parliament with unlimited legislative powers, a Parliament that is central to British conceptions of themselves. The proceedings of the House of Commons are often disorderly and theatrical. MPs are often cursed by voters. But the House of Commons reflects conflicting national emotions more accurately, I believe, than any other European legislature. Its central role in our political culture is closely associated with another unspoken instinct of great emotional power. It is that democracy is essentially national and not international. In a democracy, people have to identify themselves with a representative legislature. They need to feel that it is there to speak for them. An international legislature such as the European Parliament can only do that if the people of Europe have a European identity. You cannot create a European identity by law. Identity is a profound cultural fact. It depends on what people feel themselves to be. The word nationalism has xenophobic overtones and the history of the twentieth century has taught us to be wary of that. But Brexit is not about nationalism. It is about identity. The preamble to the European Union treaties famously refers to the desire of the European peoples to achieve an 'ever closer union'. The British have never shared that desire. This is not new. It is not the creation of Boris Johnson or Nigel Farage or any of the current generation of politicians. It goes back to the origins of the European Union and of British membership of the European Union.

Britain was not a founding member of what was then called the European Economic Community. It was not therefore involved in the creation of the union's institutional structure. That structure was essentially designed by the French, in accordance with a model that was more familiar in continental Europe than it was in Britain. The European Commission was a hybrid body, part political executive and part civil service. The power of decision ultimately lay with the Council of Ministers. There was a European Parliament, but it originally had few powers and was not at that stage directly elected. The first person to point out the dilemmas that the European project posed to Britain's traditional views about national sovereignty and democracy was Hugh Gaitskell, one of the Labour Party's outstanding post-war leaders. In a famous speech to the Labour Party conference in 1962, he made some forecasts that have proved to be prescient, and posed some important questions that were never really answered until December 2019. Gaitskell pointed out that the logic of the European project would sooner or later require decisions of the Council of Ministers to be made by a majority. When that happened, decisions of immense importance to the UK would be made by a Council of Ministers and a European Commission that would be irremovable and would not be accountable to the British Parliament, or indeed to anyone. There would be a serious democratic deficit. The designers of the European project were well aware of this criticism, and their answer was that in due course, these bodies would be accountable to the European Parliament. That would, as Gaitskell pointed out, involve the subordination of the British Parliament to a supranational legislature. 'This is what it means', he said. 'It means the end of Britain as an independent nation state. It may be a good thing or a bad thing, but we must recognise that it is so ... It means the end of a thousand years of history. You may say

"Let it end", but my goodness it is a decision that needs a little care and thought.'

Britain is not of course the only country in Europe that cares passionately about its national sovereignty. France has a very similar tradition, although in France it has usually been embodied in a powerful executive rather than in a representative assembly. But France was, and is, in a different position. In the first place, it is a country whose participation is essential to the continued existence of the European Union in a way that is true of no other European country except Germany. Secondly, French governments have had a very particular and consistent geopolitical view about the United States. They made a conscious decision in the 1960s that European integration was a price worth paying for building a powerful political and economic bloc able to deal with the United States on equal terms. They have stuck to that decision ever since. Britain, by comparison, has enduring cultural and political links with the USA that are important to us in spite of our misgivings about President Trump. Third, and crucially, the French in the 1960s and 1970s believed that European integration would enable them to dominate the European project, which at the time they largely did. That is still the motive behind French support for European integration, although I think that in a Europe of twenty-eight countries with a reunified Germany, it has become unrealistic.

In Britain, there was never an answer to Gaitskell's analysis, because the dilemma which he pointed out was simply evaded. The political leaders who made the case for European Union membership in the 1960s and early 1970s fell into two groups. There were those who believed that the aspiration to ever closer union was just rhetoric, and that it would never happen. This group has proved to be mistaken. And there were those like Edward Heath, the British prime minister who negotiated our entry, who understood the direction in which the European Union was bound to move, but believed that it would happen gradually, and that over the years a new European identity would be created which the British would accept. This group has proved to be over-optimistic. In the referendum on European Union membership held in 1975, the case made for membership was entirely about trade, and not about political integration. In the referendum campaign of 2016, it was the same. During that campaign, I was often asked by European friends who followed the campaign to explain why remainers concentrated exclusively on the economic disasters that would follow if we left. Why did they not emphasise the positive and idealistic side to the European Union? Its contribution to maintaining peace in Europe since 1945? Its role in liberating eastern Europe from Communist tyranny? Its creation of a bloc able to stand up to the United States and Russia? Its championing of democracy and liberal values? My answer was that the European Union's contribution to these things had no resonance in Britain except in the eyes of those who were already committed to remaining, and not all of them. There has never been much idealism about the European Union in Britain, even among remainers. This is partly because it is viewed as just a trading arrangement and not a political project. And it is partly because the European Union's institutions are rather unappealing: remote, undemocratic, bureaucratic and foreign. To the great majority of British voters, the question whether to leave or remain was simply a question of price. Were the institutional drawbacks, high financial contributions and loss of sovereignty a price worth paying for the economic advantages?

The British have never accepted a European identity as a substitute for their own. You do not, in England, see the European flag flying over public buildings. The language of political discourse is not European but national. Our legal system is based on the common law, a system of customary law that is the fruit of our collective experience going back many centuries and shared by no other European country except Ireland. Foreign languages have a low priority in our educational system. When direct elections to the European Parliament began in 1979, very few people bothered to vote at all. Polling figures remained low to the end. The basic problem about the European Parliament is that people do not regard it as a legitimate source of authority unless they feel that their identity is European. That is a minority position in Britain, and I believe in many European countries. Without a European Parliament that people can regard as reflecting their own identity, there is a serious democratic deficit at the heart of the European project. I do not doubt that a European identity will develop, but it will take a long time.

In Britain, these things are all symptoms of a profound national indifference to the European aspiration for 'ever closer union'. What happened over the years after Mr Cameron announced the referendum was that the British were confronted with contradictions that had existed ever since we joined. They were confronted with the most fundamental question that a community can ask itself. Who are we? The British didn't ask themselves that question when they thought that the European Union was just a trading arrangement. But in 2016 they were faced with having to make the choice that they had avoided for the previous half-century, between a national and a European identity. They chose a national one.

The origins of the modern Eurosceptic movement in Britain lie in the 1980s, in other words at precisely the time when Hugh Gaitskell's predictions were becoming a reality. The critical period was Jacques Delors' presidency of the European Commission between 1985 and 1995. Delors was a French socialist who decisively moved the European Commission into social policy, at a time when the Conservative government of Margaret Thatcher was trying to reduce the social interventions of the state in Britain. Ironically, the biggest change, the Single European Act, was an initiative of Margaret Thatcher. It was designed to remove non-tariff barriers to trade in goods and services. To do that, it was necessary to remove the veto of individual states that might be used to protect their national markets. The Single European Act was very much in Britain's economic interest as a major exporter of services. But it opened the way for a wide range of social regulations at European level, and involved a massive transfer of legislative power to the institutions of the European Union. She later regretted it. Her public repentance came with her famous Bruges speech of September 1988, an angry attack on the expanding legislative competence of the European Union beyond the field of trade. 'We have not successfully rolled back the frontiers of the state in Britain,' she said, 'only to see them re-imposed at a European level.'

Europe is an issue that cuts across party lines in Britain. But the Eurosceptic movement found its natural home in the Conservative Party, where a growing body of MPs became increasingly hostile to the centralising tendencies of the European Union. John Major, who succeeded Margaret Thatcher as prime minister in 1990, was a strong supporter of British participation in Europe, as indeed he still is. He recognised that Britain's influence in the union depended on its accepting the aspiration of other European leaders to greater political integration. But when the Maastricht Treaty was negotiated in 1992, with its provisions for monetary union, he was confronted for the first time with treaty proposals that he would not be able to sell to his own party or, in all probability, to Parliament. Monetary union presented

Britain with a difficult dilemma. It was an economic project that was adopted by Europe for political reasons, not economic ones. It could not work without a large measure of political integration in Europe and the loss of an important tool of economic management by national governments. The dilemma was put off by negotiating a British opt-out from the single currency. But that was only a partial solution. The Eurozone would inevitably become a centre of European decision-making in which Britain, as a non-Euro country, would have little if any influence. The whole issue of monetary union brought to a head the conflict between the economic and the political view of the European project, although it fell to the Labour government which took office in 1997 to resolve it. The new prime minister, Tony Blair, wanted to join the Euro. He wanted it for essentially political reasons. He believed that it would increase British influence in Europe and that it would help to create a European identity in Britain. Gordon Brown, the powerful Chancellor of the Exchequer, supported by senior officials in the Treasury, was unwilling to address the issue in any but economic terms. He considered that the UK should not adopt the Euro unless certain economic tests were satisfied. They were never satisfied, and never likely to be satisfied. In a sense Blair and Brown were both right. Blair was right on the political plane, and Brown was right on the economic one. The whole affair encapsulated the British dilemma. Brown won. The economic prevailed over the political once more.

The crunch came under the Tory government of David Cameron, who became prime minister in 2010. Cameron had not achieved an absolute majority in the election of 2010. He was obliged to govern in coalition with the Liberal Democrats, who were wholly committed to a European future for the United Kingdom. So was Cameron personally, but a large minority of his party was not. The Eurosceptic wing had by now become unmanageably powerful and threatened to tear the Tory party apart. Successive Conservative governments had managed the problem by keeping the issue of our continued membership off the political agenda. But that became increasingly difficult as a result of the rise of the UK Independence Party (UKIP), led by Nigel Farage, a former Conservative whose views had great appeal to much of the Tory party's electoral base. The only way out was a referendum. Cameron was confident that he would win it, and that that would silence the Eurosceptics in his own party. He was wrong on both counts. The Eurosceptics in the Tory party would not have been silenced if he had won, and UKIP certainly would not have been silenced. But in fact, he did not win. The offer of a choice about European Union membership unleashed years of frustrated resentment of the European Union among people who suddenly realised that there was something that they could do about it. Their frustration was magnified by the refusal of the other European Union countries to make any significant concession to Mr Cameron of a kind that might have made it easier for him to sell Europe to the public. The rest of Europe perceived that Mr Cameron's negotiating position was a bluff. They thought that he would campaign to remain even if they conceded nothing. They were right about that. Their mistake was that they never took seriously the possibility that the British might leave over Mr Cameron's dead body.

David Cameron is often accused of gambling his country's future in the interests of the unity of the Tory party. There is some truth in that. But one has to remember how political parties function in a democracy. Politics is a marketplace. Political parties are coalitions of opinion united by a loose consistency of outlook and the desire to win elections. They operate as the essential link between the electorate and government. It is their proper function to adapt their policies to persistent changes in the sentiments of the electorate in the interest of getting elected. That is how democracy works. The Tory party is the oldest and most successful machine for winning elections in European history. Its intellectual origins lie in the early eighteenth century. It has been an organised party since the 1830s and has had a national organisation since the 1870s. It has been in power for most of the time since then. Its success is due chiefly to its ability to adapt to changing public expectations. The dilemmas of the Tory party about Europe over the past forty years have in a real sense been the dilemmas of Britain as a whole. They are shared by many supporters of the Labour Party. That is perhaps the most striking lesson of the 2019 general election. The result was due mainly to a gut feeling, shared by a significant body of Labour as well as Tory voters, that national identity mattered and that it was threatened by a European project which could only succeed by diluting national sovereignty. They showed this not just by voting for the only party unequivocally committed to Brexit, but by rejecting the Labour leader Jeremy Corbyn. Corbyn was a deeply unpopular figure among traditional Labour voters. His support for a second referendum was only part of the problem. Corbyn's support for various revolutionary movements in Ireland, South America and Palestine, and his persistent criticism of British military and intelligence operations, offended the innate patriotism of Labour's traditional working-class supporters. It offended the same instincts that made them object to the European Union. They felt sufficiently strongly about it to cross party lines on a scale unprecedented in modern British politics.

I profoundly disagree with the decision of my fellow countrymen to leave the European Union. But I can understand and even empathise with their reasons. I myself feel the attractions of autonomy and national sovereignty. I too am influenced by the radical differences between our history and political culture and those of the rest of Europe. I was a remainer because I believed, and still believe, that Britain will be dominated by the European Union whether we belong to it or not. We are geographically part of Europe. Our social values are European. Europe is our largest market. If we are going to be dominated by the European Union anyway, we might as well have a voice in its decisions. There are, moreover, many challenges such as climate change or the regulation of monopolies that can only be handled at international level. Autonomy is emotionally attractive, but there is not much that you can do with it in an interdependent world in which power comes from membership of large economic and political blocs. Far from taking back control, I believe that leaving the European Union will reduce our control over our own lives and fortunes. I also think that it is fundamentally wrong for the older generation to shut the door on a project which most younger people, who will have to live with the consequences for longer, want to belong to.

So what of the future? I am not a prophet, and anyway prophets are usually wrong. But let me make a number of points.

The first is that the paralysis and near breakdown of British politics which we witnessed between 2016 and 2019 was highly uncharacteristic of British politics and it will not continue. It was the result of a combination of some most unusual factors. In a parliamentary system, a referendum can only work if it is about a precisely formulated draft law, which can automatically come into force if the answer is Yes. This is the way that referendums work in France and Switzerland. The referendum of 2016 left most of the difficult questions unanswered for Parliament to deal with. It also put pressure on Members of Parliament to pay lip service to Brexit, because although most of them did not believe in it, their electors did. The result was that Parliament was as divided as the people that they represented. Unfortunately, this happened at a time when we had a minority government, a rare event in British history. Mrs May was at the mercy of a well-organised group of extreme anti-Europeans in her own party who sunk every deal that she made, and a smaller but highly effective group of remainers who joined forces with the Labour Party to deprive her government of control over the parliamentary agenda. A similar combination of circumstances is unlikely to arise again.

My second point about the future is this. The referendum and the recent election occurred at an unfortunate moment in the development of our relations with the European Union. I have argued that a European identity is an essential requirement for the European project to succeed. The lack of it in Britain was the main reason for British resentment of the expanding political agenda of the European Union. But until recently there were signs of a European identity beginning to emerge among the young, even in Britain. About 70 per cent of those under twenty-five voted to remain, compared with only 40 per cent of those over sixty-five. The younger generation are much less respectful of our parliamentary culture and more internationalist in outlook. In the longer term, therefore, Euroscepticism was bound to be a declining force. As time went on, the number of leavers would decline as they died off and more young people come into the electorate. Without the referendum of 2016, I think it very likely that Euroscepticism would have become a marginal factor in British politics within ten years. During that time, our influence in the European Union would have increased, because population projections suggest that by 2030 Britain will be the most populous country in Europe by quite a large margin. It is now, unfortunately, too late, because we left before these changes could bear fruit. In theory, we might apply to rejoin.

But in practice that seems most unlikely. Rejoining would require Britain to accept the *acquis Communautaire*, the accumulated powers and practices of the European institutions. Without Britain, the European Union is likely to evolve in ways that will be more alien and less acceptable to our people. As time goes on this will make it progressively harder for us to rejoin.

Third, in the long term what sort of relationship can we expect between Britain and the European Union? It is I think unlikely that Britain will try to compete for investment with Europe by adopting a lower level of social provision. The British love affair with neo-liberal economics is over. The British electorate demands high levels of social provision, just as European electorates do. That is particularly true of voters in the constituencies that the Conservatives have just taken from Labour in the Midlands and north of England, which they are desperate to keep. It is quite likely that we will compete with Europe in other areas, notably business taxation, business regulation and trade relations with third countries. Indeed, we have already begun to do so. This may prove to be an obstacle to an acceptable trading agreement with the EU after we leave. But I think that it would be a serious mistake for the European Union to adopt its traditional negotiating technique of simply offering an off-the-shelf solution on a take it or leave it basis. That would risk creating an economically powerful but permanently hostile and resentful Britain on Europe's doorstep, which would not be in the interests of either side.

Finally, what are we to make of the Johnson government? Boris Johnson is a controversial figure in England, as he is in Europe. To his many enemies he has become something of a bogeyman. In the German press, notably in *Der Spiegel*, he is often treated as a figure of fun. This is a mistake. Johnson is an intensely ambitious politician and a skilful campaigner.

He was not a good foreign secretary and he has yet to show that he can run a government. A lot may depend on the qualities of his ministers. The fact that they appear to have been chosen exclusively for their loyalty to him and their belief in Brexit does not augur well. By background and instinct, Johnson is a liberal, but he is above all an opportunist and he knows that a neo-liberal agenda will not get him re-elected. He is certainly not another Donald Trump. So far as Johnson has any real political convictions, he is essentially a British Gaullist with a Christian Democratic social programme. His large majority in the House of Commons has put him in a position of great personal power in Britain. This, and his lack of any strong personal principles, seem likely to make him a highly flexible negotiator who may well end up conceding much of the EU's negotiating demands. He is quite good at negotiating a surrender and dressing it up as a victory. Johnson's hero is Winston Churchill. But among former British prime ministers, the one that he most resembles is not Churchill. It is the nineteenth-century Tory politician Benjamin Disraeli. Disraeli was an outsider, an ambitious adventurer and an unscrupulous opportunist, who split his party and came close to destroying it in his pursuit of personal power. Politically, his contemporaries regarded him as totally amoral, very much as people now regard Boris Johnson. Yet he was also the architect of the modern Tory party, the inventor of the phrase 'one nation conservatism' and, as it turned out, an excellent prime minister.

This piece was originally a lecture delivered to German judges at the Federal Judicial Academy in Trier in 19 December 2019, shortly after the British general election had returned a Conservative government with an absolute majority and a mandate to 'Get Brexit Done'. It is presented here substantially as delivered.

10

BREXIT AND THE BRITISH
CONSTITUTION

When Walter Bagehot wrote the second edition of his classic account of the British Constitution in 1873 he observed that it was likely to be out of date very quickly. The British Constitution under Lord Palmerston, which he had described in the first edition, was very different from that of Benjamin Disraeli only a decade later. In the absence of a written code or comprehensive legal rules, the British Constitution is whatever happens. As Bagehot put it, the constitution 'has continued in outward sameness but in hidden inner change.' He regarded this as an advantage. It enabled the constitution to adapt to external shocks. But it meant that, as so often in Britain, the label does not always match the contents of the bottle. It also enables the British to achieve major constitutional changes by accident, without necessarily intending it. Does this matter? It is far from clear that we would have a better constitution if we changed it on purpose. We would certainly have a much more rigid one. I very much doubt whether a more formal constitution would have weathered the crisis of the past three years as well as the one we have.

During that period the constitution has undergone significant changes, most of which can be traced to the decision to leave the European Union. They include major changes in the role of political parties, in the relations of the government with Parliament, and in the constitutional role of the courts. All of them have been controversial. But the controversy was distorted by the European debate. People welcomed or deplored the changes, depending on how they affected the likelihood of our leaving the EU, and where they stood on that issue. This is, to my mind, rather absurd. Ultimately constitutional change must be considered on its merits, irrespective of our views about any particular political issue. The questions which I want to address here are: why the decision to leave the EU provoked the biggest constitutional crisis of our recent history and what continuing effect that crisis will have on public life now that it is over, at any rate at a domestic political level.

The Brexit crisis was the combined result of three remarkable developments. The first was the attempt to resolve a highly controversial question by introducing an element of direct democracy into a parliamentary system. The second was the advent of a minority government. And the third was the collapse of a shared political culture. These three things were of course related. The starting point for all three of them was the referendum.

A referendum is a device for circumventing the parliamentary process. The justification for doing that in 2016 was that there was a mismatch between parliamentary sentiment and public opinion. Public opinion was divided on the European Union, but all parties represented in Parliament believed that we should remain in it. So if you wanted to leave, there was no party that you could vote for except for UKIP, which had no MPs and little prospect of getting any. In due course, this problem would probably have resolved itself. Sooner or later, the transformation of the Conservative Party into an anti-EU party would, I think, have occurred anyway, as a result of the growth of anti-European sentiment among its electoral base. But David Cameron's decision to try to lance the boil in 2016 accelerated the process, with highly disruptive consequences. The great Victorian constitutional lawyer A. V. Dicey, whose works are still authoritative, was a believer in referendums. He thought that they were a superior alternative to party politics, which he regarded as a source of unnecessary strife and division. He argued that referendums were a useful way of restraining the wild projects of politicians. A referendum, he said, was 'an emphatic assertion of the principle that nation stands above party'. It would be hard to imagine a clearer refutation of Dicey's view than the referendum of 2016. The argument does not work if it is the nation that is divided, rather than the parties.

There were two things wrong with the referendum of 2016. The first is common to all referendums on issues about which there are strong feelings. They create a sense of entitlement in the majority that inhibits compromise and invites absolute outcomes. This is the mentality summed up in the oft-repeated statement that 'the British people' had voted to leave the EU. It implied what many people said out loud, that the 48 per cent who voted to stay were not for this purpose to be regarded as part of the British people and did not count. Far from uniting the nation as Dicey envisaged, the referendum of 2016 sundered the four nations of the United Kingdom. It divided us by class, by region, by economic status and by generation. It split families and alienated friends. It poisoned our politics. It was the most significant single cause of the demise of the shared political culture that had hitherto enabled our constitution to work. That has in turn encouraged resort to a much more authoritarian style of government.

The second objection is specific to the referendum of 2016. In countries such as France and Switzerland the constitutions of which provide for referendums, it is necessary to formulate a precise legislative proposal the approval of which by the electorate will be decisive. This was the kind of referendum that Dicey supported. It was the kind of referendum that Britain itself chose for the Scottish devolution referendum of 1979 and the alternative vote referendum of 2011. The problem with the question asked in 2016 is that there were too many answers to it other than Yes or No. You might be in favour of leaving the EU in any circumstances whatever. Some people were. Or you might be in favour of leaving it only on the footing urged by the Leave campaign, namely that a satisfactory agreement could easily be reached about future relations with the EU. If that was your view, there were any number of different kinds of agreement with the EU that you might regard as satisfactory. Unfortunately, the nature of our future relations with the EU after leaving was not on the ballot paper. It hardly could have been, since it depended on the result of a future negotiation. Yet that was the whole subject of dispute for the next three and a half years. The referendum might have been decisive if the answer had been Remain, although I doubt it. If the answer was Leave, all the difficult questions would be left unanswered for Parliament to deal with. As a result, the referendum was not the end of the argument, but only the beginning. Against that background, it is very odd to say that Parliament had no business to be arguing about Brexit.

Yet that is what the government did say. The House of Commons was repeatedly accused of obstructing the attempt to implement the result of the referendum. This accusation reached the outer limits of hyperbole in September 2019 when the attorney-general (of all people) told the House of Commons that it had 'no moral right to sit'. In its manifesto for the subsequent election, the Conservative Party declared that MPs had 'devoted themselves to thwarting the democratic decision of the British people in the 2016 referendum'. This sort of thing has been repeated so often that we are in danger of believing it. Yet it is manifestly untrue. The facts are that the House of Commons voted by a very large majority to serve the Article 50 notice terminating British membership of the Union within two years. It accepted the principle of leaving the EU. But on the terms of our departure it was as divided as the population that it served, as was only proper. The real burden of the government's complaint against Parliament was that a majority of MPs was unwilling to allow them to leave the EU until they had made satisfactory alternative arrangements. This undoubtedly weakened the government's negotiating hand in Brussels, but it was neither unreasonable nor undemocratic.

Having sponsored a referendum that left Parliament to sort out all the uncertainties and ambiguities of the result, the government then called a general election in May 2017 and lost the majority that might have enabled that to be achieved. There had been minority governments before 2017: between February and October 1974; in the last two years of the Callaghan administration from 1977 to 1979; and in the final months of John Major's administration in 1997. The brief Labour administrations of the 1920s were minority governments, which was the source of most of their problems. Otherwise, you have to go back to the nineteenth century to find a minority administration. In each case, the situation was managed by avoiding controversial legislation. But that was hardly possible for Mrs May, because Brexit, one of the most controversial policies ever espoused by a British government, was top of the agenda. The result of all this was to test to the edge of destruction some of the basic principles on which our constitution works.

Britain is a parliamentary democracy in a more fundamental sense than is commonly realised. It is not just that, like every other democracy, we have a representative legislature. The whole structure of our institutions depends on Parliament being the ultimate decision-maker. This is because of the way in which our democracy evolved out of a monarchical constitution. Walter Bagehot described Britain as a 'disguised republic'. The Crown has extraordinarily wide prerogative powers, whose actual exercise by the monarch would be quite inconsistent with a democratic constitution. In theory, the monarch appoints and dismisses ministers. In theory, the monarch summons, dissolves and prorogues Parliament. In theory, the monarch consents to parliamentary legislation, without which it is not valid. In theory, the monarch conducts the international relations of the United Kingdom. These relics of absolute monarchy have been limited by convention since the eighteenth century. By convention, the prerogative powers of the Crown are actually exercised by her ministers, who are answerable for their exercise to Parliament. By convention, the monarch must appoint ministers who command the confidence of the House of Commons and may not retain the services of ministers who have lost it. By convention, the monarch does not veto parliamentary legislation. We are only a democracy because of these conventions. Their combined effect is that the legitimacy of governmental action depends on parliamentary sentiment. In overtly presidential constitutions like those of the United States or France there are constitutional documents from which the executive can derive legitimacy for its acts, independent of the legislature. There is nothing equivalent in Britain.

This is, admittedly, not how most people think about the matter. In general elections, most people do not regard themselves as voting for an MP. They regard themselves as voting for a government. Parliament is just part of the mechanics for giving effect to their choice. But there are obvious reasons why it is important to stick to the constitutional view and not the popular one. One reason is that the popular view does not work even in its own terms. Very few British governments have come to power with an absolute majority of the votes cast. They have almost all been minority governments in electoral terms. But the first-past-the-post system in parliamentary elections commonly means that they have an absolute majority in parliamentary terms. There is, however, a more fundamental reason. The diversity of opinions among MPs, even within a single political party, is an important part of the process by which governments achieve the broadest possible basis of consent for their acts. The popular view of the electoral process would confer despotic power on ministers, constrained only by their fear of retribution at the polls at the next election, which may be a long way off.

Constitutional conventions are accepted rules of practice which are not necessarily legally binding, but which it would be politically costly to ignore. The dependence of our constitution on conventions is often presented as a British peculiarity. In fact, all constitutions depend to some extent on conventions. Law is never enough. Even in a highly formal and law-based constitution like that of the United States, the importance of conventions becomes obvious when you see what happens when they are cast aside, as they have been by President Trump. The world is full of countries whose democratic constitutions have been subverted entirely legally by governments set on exploiting legal forms to undermine democratic substance: Chile, Peru, Venezuela, Hungary, Turkey, Russia. The list gets longer every year. But although conventions matter everywhere, they are particularly important in an informal and political constitution such as the British one. In our system, they are the main barrier against the ministerial despotism that would otherwise be implicit in our quasi-monarchical constitution. The problem about constitutional conventions is that they depend on a shared political culture. A shared political culture means the mutual acceptance that the constitution must be made to work in the interests not just of one side but of the system as a whole. It means a common sentiment about what are the limits of political propriety. It means that not everything that legally can be done, should be done. All of this requires a culture that accepts pluralism and diversity of opinion; in which opponents are not enemies but fellow citizens who disagree and with whom it is necessary to engage.

Faced with a Parliament that rejected their blueprint for relations with the EU after Brexit, both Mrs May's and Mr Johnson's governments claimed an alternative source of constitutional legitimacy, displacing Parliament, based on the result of the referendum. The constitution showed itself to be remarkably resilient in the face of this threat to the fundamental assumptions on which it operates. Its flexibility enabled it to fight back on two main fronts. One was the procedures of the House of Commons. They were significantly changed by Speaker Bercow with the support of a majority of the House, including an important group within the governing party. The other was the courts. They gave legal effect to the traditional understanding of the role of Parliament, which the government believed to be a mere matter of convention and which it had resolved to disregard.

The procedures of the House of Commons are one of the most arcane parts of our constitution. But they are of critical importance. They determine in important respects the relationship between the government and the legislature. The British Parliament is unusual among democratic legislatures. It is not just a lawmaker and an external check on government. It is itself an instrument of government. Its main function is to support the government, or change it for another which it can support. This is reflected in the fact that in the Westminster model, unlike other legislative models, ministers actually sit in Parliament. Together with their parliamentary private secretaries, they currently comprise about a fifth of the House of Commons. It is also reflected in the fact that the ministry is selected for its numbers in the House. And it is reflected in the House's rules. Standing Order 14 of the House provides that with limited exceptions 'government business shall have precedence at every sitting'. Since at least the beginning of the twentieth century, the parliamentary agenda has been decided by the government. The Leader of the House, a government minister, puts forward business motions. The opposition cannot normally put forward its own business motions or amend the government's. These procedures do not sit well with minority government. Their whole basis and their sole justification is the assumption that the government commands a sufficient majority in the House of Commons to get its business through. The government in the last Parliament was in a different and unusual position. The House of Commons professed to have confidence in Her Majesty's government but not in its only significant policy. In the face of this difficulty, Mrs May's government engaged in what can only be described as a crude piece of blackmail. It tried to force MPs to support its own proposals by using its control over the parliamentary agenda to stifle consideration of anyone else's. The calculation was that in the face of the Article 50 deadline and the risks of a no-deal exit, MPs would be forced to submit.

This tactic was circumvented by Speaker Bercow. Bercow was a controversial figure. He was rude, loud and excessively talkative. But this country owes him a very great debt. He adapted the procedures of the House of Commons to accommodate the problems provoked by a minority government. The Speaker is the servant of the House of Commons. It is not his job to make things easier for a government whose policies do not have the support of the House. In December

2018 Bercow departed from normal practice by allowing MPs to amend government business motions and put forward their own programme. In September 2019, during the brief period between the return of Parliament from its recess and its prorogation a week later, the government deliberately declined to move any business motions so as to frustrate any attempt to amend them in this way. Bercow responded by allowing private members to take control of the order paper under Standing Order 24, which provides for emergency debates. The Speaker allowed it to be used to make time for the so-called Benn Act to be tabled and passed, which forced the prime minister to apply for an extension of the deadline for negotiations. Both of these innovations left the government speechless with rage. But both were necessary to cope with the problems of having a minority government in a representative democracy.

Baulked by the Speaker's inventive approach to procedure, the government resorted to proroguing Parliament. That provoked what was perhaps the most controversial of all the constitutional developments arising from the Brexit crisis, namely the intervention of the courts. Prorogation was a more significant step in September 2019 than it would normally have been. Normally a major change in our law requires positive action from Parliament. But under Article 50 of the EU Treaty, if Parliament did nothing Britain would automatically leave the EU on 31 October 2019 with or without a satisfactory agreement. The prorogation of Parliament was conceived as a way of ensuring that Parliament did nothing for long enough to achieve this seismic change, notwithstanding strong parliamentary opposition to it. As it happened, this result was prevented by the so-called Benn Act, which was passed in a great hurry after the government announced its plan to prorogue. But if the government had been right on the question of principle, and had had sufficient foresight, it could have prevented the Benn Act by proroguing Parliament earlier.

The government's decision to prorogue Parliament was not exactly a breach of convention. The power of prorogation was an ancient power dating back to the medieval origins of Parliament. It had historically been exercised for a wide variety of reasons, including political ones. In England, John Major prorogued Parliament in 1997 in order to forestall a debate on the cash-for-questions scandal. More recently, in 2008, the prime minister of Canada, Stephen Harper, prorogued Parliament in order to pre-empt a motion of no confidence, after his coalition partners deserted him and joined the opposition, thereby depriving him of his majority. The Governor-General of Canada had misgivings about what she was being asked to do. But the step was never challenged in the courts. As is well known, it was successfully challenged in this country. But if prorogation was not a breach of convention, it was clearly a gross breach of the shared political culture that placed Parliament at the centre of the political system. It was a direct assertion of executive power to force through a policy that Parliament did not support and was not prepared to authorise. In the event the Johnson government's object was frustrated partly by the Benn Act and partly by the Supreme Court.

There was no doubt that in principle an exercise of the royal prerogative can be judicially reviewed. That was decided in a famous case before the Law Lords in 1984 involving the decision to ban trades unions at the Government Communications Headquarters.[16] However, for an exercise of the prerogative (or any other ministerial decision) to be quashed, there must be some legal criterion by which it can be found wanting. Political outrage is not enough. So the decision to prorogue Parliament faced the Supreme Court with a question as fundamental as any that a British court has ever had to consider. The sole basis on which we are entitled to call ourselves a parliamentary democracy is that governments are answerable to Parliament. The question was whether this was a principle of law, and therefore binding, or a mere matter of political sentiment, which the government was at liberty to ignore. The Court held that it was a principle of law. Mr Rees-Mogg, the leader of the House, is said to have described this as a 'constitutional coup'. This strikes me as rather extravagant. The prime minister is a public officer. The power to prorogue Parliament is a public power. The common law has always been reluctant to recognise that a public officer can exercise a public power without being accountable to anyone but himself: not to the monarch, because in practice he is himself exercising the monarch's powers; not to the electorate because the electorate has no institutional means of holding the government to account otherwise than through Parliament; not to Parliament because it will have been prorogued. The effect, if the government had been right, would have been to transform a public power into a personal privilege of the prime minister.

I have been a critic of the tendency of the courts to arrogate to themselves decisions that are properly matters for political debate and parliamentary accountability. But this was different. The Supreme Court intervened not to claim decision-making powers for judges but to safeguard the decision-making powers of Parliament. It reminded us that under our constitution the government's sole source of legitimacy is the support of the House of Commons. This was something that the government had been inclined to overlook. In former times, the question would have been resolved in accordance with a shared understanding of the political community about the limits of political propriety. But what happens if that understanding breaks down? Do the courts simply stand by and say 'Oh dear!'? Some, perhaps most, conventional assumptions about politics do not lend themselves to judicial enforcement. But others are so fundamental to the democratic character of our constitution that their destruction would leave an intolerable void. This was such a case.

By September 2019, the impossibility of sidelining Parliament and the absence of a majority in Parliament for any alternative solution to the European conundrum had combined to bring the business of the moment to a standstill. The traditional safety valve in this situation is a dissolution and a general election. Walter Bagehot described this as an appeal from one Parliament to the next. In words that might have been written for the prime minister, he wrote that the government was entitled to say: 'You Members of Parliament are not doing your duty. You are gratifying caprice at the cost of the nation. You are indulging party spirit at the cost of the nation. You are helping yourself at the cost of the nation. I will see whether the nation approves what you are doing or not; I will appeal from Parliament No. 1 to Parliament No. 2.' Brexit was the major issue at the resultant election. The scale of the Conservative victory conferred democratic legitimacy on the government's Brexit policy, something that the referendum had never done. The referendum campaign had been fought in a fog of ignorance and a cacophony of tendentious and unverifiable claims and counterclaims about what the consequences of leaving might be. It had signally failed to address the question of our future relations with the EU. None of this was true of the general election of December 2019. The governing party's intentions were clear, and so were their political and economic implications. We are not obliged to agree with the decision to leave the European Union. But we do have to accept that it is what most of our fellow citizens want, whatever the consequences.

With an overall majority of eighty, the government will not now need to play fast and loose with constitutional principle in order to get its way. It would be agreeable to think that, as a result, the breakdown of our political culture in the past three years was just a passing phase. Unfortunately, there are signs that this may be too optimistic.

The first of them concerns the organisation of political parties. Political parties have a critical function in a parliamentary democracy. Politics is a marketplace. Parties mediate between the public and the state in their search for a slate of policies that can attract the widest range of support and maximise their electoral prospects. But the political market has taken a serious knock over the past few years. The problem arises mainly from the tiny membership rolls of the constituency associations which constitute the basic units of political parties. This has happened over a long period – more than fifty years. It has happened partly as a result in changes of patterns of sociability that have made local political associations less significant in the social life of our population; and partly as a result of the more fickle and less tribal allegiance of most voters. But the ironic result of people becoming less tribal is that political parties have become more so. Because of the dwindling membership rolls of constituency associations, it is too easy for small but well-organised groups to take over political parties, as Momentum has taken over much of the Labour Party and UKIP and the Brexit Party much of the Conservative Party. Constituency associations have immense power. They select parliamentary candidates. They make the ultimate choice of the party's leader in the House of Commons. Entryists are almost by definition activists and zealots. They narrow the party's policy offering. This limits the choices available to the electorate to relatively extreme positions. The problem is particularly acute when it happens to both major parties at the same time.

In a famous lecture in 1976, Lord Hailsham described the British Constitution as an 'elective dictatorship'.[17] This, he said, was because of the immense power possessed by a government with an overall majority in the House of Commons. Lord Hailsham was I think wrong in 1976. He looked only at the mechanics of party discipline in the House of Commons, and not at the process by which party policy is made. Traditionally, political parties have been 'big tents' or 'broad churches'. They have not been cramped bunkers or narrow sects. The operation of the political market means that party policy is usually a compromise: not just a compromise between different groups within the party, but a compromise with the policy platforms of other parties whose clothes it is electorally desirable to steal. This is how the political market works. It is fundamental to the ability of a democracy to accommodate dissent and enable us to live together in a single political community. It is why the narrowing of the intellectual base of both major parties is such a significant development. By limiting the electorate's choices to relatively extreme positions, the polarisation of politics disables the political market and obstructs the process by which we accommodate dissent. It means that Lord Hailsham's warning about elective dictators, which was not justified in his day, may shortly be justified in ours.

The polarisation of politics has proved destructive of the way that politics accommodates a wide range of opinion. It is also symptomatic of something more sinister, which I hope it is not too melodramatic to call a developing totalitarian tendency. There has been a growing intolerance of dissent and a tendency to deny the legitimacy of opposition. Let us look at the signs.

First, there was the consistent habit during the prolonged Brexit crisis of shooting the messenger without engaging with the message. The governor of the Bank of England, the British Permanent Representative to the EU, the civil service authors of various projections of the economic impact of

Brexit, the assumptions underlying Operation Yellowhammer (the contingency plan for a no-deal Brexit), have all expressed views based on the careful analysis of evidence. None of them have been met with a reasoned or evidence-based refutation. Instead, they were summarily rejected for no other reason than that they did not suit the public position of those who wished to leave the EU come what may. The authors, it was said, must be remainers. Therefore one need not engage with their views. In the case of the governor of the Bank of England, it was seriously suggested by Mr Rees-Mogg that he had no business to be expressing a view at all.

Second, there was the expulsion of twenty-one MPs from the Conservative Party for failing to support the government in its willingness to risk a no-deal exit in its negotiations with the EU. They were prevented from fighting the election as the Conservatives that they undoubtedly were. All of those who tried to fight their seats as independents were defeated by more compliant government candidates. This was not an ordinary measure of party discipline. It was a political purge. Of course, political parties have always had this power. But they have recoiled from using it in order to keep their electoral appeal as broad as possible. The present government fought the last election on the basis that they did not need a broad appeal because the polarisation of politics would enable them to win without one. As it turned out, they were right about that. This has been mainly an issue in the Conservative Party, but the Labour Party has not been far behind. In July 2019, it was reported that seventy Labour MPs thought to be hostile to Momentum were facing the threat of deselection. They were saved from this ordeal by the early onset of the general election. This kind of approach from dominant groups in both major parties suggests that the extraordinarily narrow political base of the constituency associations is already leading to a more authoritarian political style.

Third, there was the present government's successful but disreputable argument that Parliament and the courts were frustrating the will of the people. This was an attempt to capitalise on anti-political feelings that have been mounting in most western democracies for many years. But whatever we may think of our politicians, we cannot have liberty without democracy, or democracy without politics, or politics without politicians. To denounce politics as anti-democratic is not just a contradiction in terms. It is bound to lead to a more authoritarian style of government which we will not like.

Fourth, there is the attack on the judiciary. The prime minister has said that his proposals will distinguish between judicial review designed to protect ordinary citizens from oppressive governmental acts, and judicial review which is really politics by other means. As I sought to explain in my Reith Lectures, there is a real problem about judicial review. It has tended to intrude into areas that properly belong to Parliament and to ministers answerable to Parliament. Unfortunately this part of the government's programme seems to have been provoked by resentment of the Supreme Court's decisions in the two Gina Miller cases, which turned on a quite different issue. Those decisions did not involve the judicial usurpation of the role of Parliament. On the contrary, both of them defended Parliament against an executive that wanted to sideline it.

When the government loses a judicial review it is invariably because it is found to have acted illegally, or to have done something that it had no power to do. I do not suppose that the present government intends to introduce legislation saying that if ministers act illegally or without legal power, the courts must not intervene if they did it for political reasons. The problem lies not in the existence of these judicial powers, which are essential in any civilised society.

It lies in the enthusiasm of some judges to find that the government has acted illegally or without power, when the real basis of their intervention is simply that they disapprove of the policies in question. I think that a change of judicial attitudes is long overdue. But you cannot achieve that by Act of Parliament. You cannot have a statute that says that judges must be more respectful in future of the proper province of politics. The only way to stop courts from holding that ministers have acted illegally or without legal power is to give ministers unlimited powers.

It is no doubt difficulties like these that explain the attorney-general's call for a political element in the appointment or confirmation of judges. To appreciate the oddity of this suggestion, you have to imagine what questions might be asked of candidates. There would be no point in asking them whether they were judicial activists. They would simply answer that they would be as active as the law and the facts of the case required them to be, no more and no less. You could ask them whether they were Tories. Or leavers. That would produce the kind of discreditable consequences that we have seen in the United States, where judges are identified with the political positions of their appointers. Indeed, that would seem to be the object of the exercise. But would the present government be happy to face a bench of judges selected on overtly political grounds by the Labour ministers who were in power from 1997 to 2010, or confirmed by the predominantly Labour parliaments of that period? This is one of the most ill-thought-out ideas ever to emerge from a resentful government frustrated by its inability to do whatever it likes. It would gravely undermine public confidence in the judicial function. And it would deter any lawyer of stature from applying for appointment. Better to continue in independent practice, they will say, and conserve their self-respect than participate in such a charade of independence.

Finally, there are the minor pointers, the straws in the wind that are sometimes as revealing as major policy statements. The government has threatened the financial model of the BBC. It is doing this at a time when it is accusing the broadcaster of a bias towards the liberal instincts that the Conservative Party is busily trying to cut out of its heritage. Ministers have conducted an organised boycott of the *Today* programme. They have refused to countenance a peerage for John Bercow, contrary to long-standing tradition, mainly on the ground that he stopped a minority government behaving as if it had a majority. This is an act of vindictive mean-mindedness unworthy of Her Majesty's government. All these are symptoms of a frame of mind uncomfortable with dissent, which feels that it is the duty of every national institution to stand behind the government.

The prime minister has declared his intention of reuniting Britain after the long Brexit crisis. This is an admirable objective, but it is unrealistic to think that it can be achieved by the combative style that we are used to hearing in statements emerging from Downing Street. People hardly ever unite around a policy, least of all one as controversial as Brexit. The only thing that ever has or ever will unite us is a common loyalty to a way of conducting our affairs that we can respect even if we disagree about the outcome. This means a process of decision-making that accommodates dissent, debate and a diversity of values. It means a process that recognises the legitimacy of opposition. It means a government which does not believe that the ends justify any means that are calculated to achieve them. These are not just optional extras or rules of courtesy. They are fundamental to the survival of the democratic state. Aristotle's objection to democracy was that it was inherently unstable. It transmuted naturally into tyranny. It is not law or constitutions that have prevented this from happening in the century and a half during which democracy has been the prevailing system in Europe and North America. It is a shared political culture. Like most cultural phenomena, a shared political culture is a spontaneous growth. It is difficult to create. But it is very easy to destroy.

This essay was a lecture delivered in January 2020 at the Oxford Martin School, a public policy institute of Oxford University, under the title 'British politics after Brexit: Reflections on the last three years and the next fifty'. An earlier version had been delivered to the Fellowship of All Souls College, where I was a Visiting Fellow at the time.

BRITAIN IN THE TWENTIES: THE
FUTURE OF THE CONSTITUTION

Nations, like people, are prisoners of their past. It was Karl Marx who put it best. 'Men make their own history,' he wrote; 'but they do not make it just as they please. They do not make it under circumstances of their own choosing, but under circumstances ... transmitted from the past.' So it is with constitutions. A constitution is the product of a nation's experience, and in ordering a nation's affairs, experience counts for more than theory. Even the most formal and elaborate constitutional codes are soon overlaid by a body of practice, convention and tradition, which is necessary to make it work. Nowhere is this truer than in Britain. Our constitution famously lacks any formal or elaborate code. It is an organic growth from our past, a reflection of our evolving political culture. It works because it goes with the grain of our history, and because it is adaptable enough to accommodate unforeseen future change. Its basic framework has survived for longer than any other national constitution in the world. This is not an accident.

If we were to decide to have a written, by which I mean a codified, constitution, all bets would be off. An essay like this, which seeks to peer into an uncertain future, would be pointless. But I take it as my starting point that this country will not have a codified constitution for the foreseeable future.

A codified constitution would have three notable disadvantages. First, it would address yesterday's problems, which we know about; but it would not address tomorrow's, unless it were framed at such a high level of generality as to leave most of the difficult questions unresolved for later. It will not therefore avoid the uncertainties for which our present constitutional arrangements are commonly criticised. Second, if a constitution is to define and limit the powers of the various organs of the state, it must be difficult to amend. It must require some special procedure, such as a supermajority in Parliament or a referendum. The result would be more rigid and less adaptable than our current arrangements. At a time when our world is likely to undergo significant social and technical change, this would be unwise. Third, it would greatly increase the political role of courts of law in our constitution. They would have to be charged with the task of interpreting highly general provisions, and filling in the inevitable gaps. This would undermine both the integrity of the political system and the standing of the judiciary. I do not detect in my fellow citizens any appetite for these things. The arguments in favour of them are purely theoretical and have no resonance among the population at large.

The central feature of the British Constitution as it stands is the sovereignty of Parliament. It is the supreme legislative and political organ of the state. The government is not directly elected, as the chief executive is in presidential constitutions like those of France or the United States. In Britain, the government's sole source of legitimacy is the support of a majority of the House of Commons. Until the Supreme Court's decision in the prorogation case last year, this was thought to be purely a matter of convention. But what was striking, even before that decision, was how resilient the convention proved to be in the face of a direct assault by a government that did not command a majority in the House of Commons. When the government of Mrs May tried to abuse the procedures of the House of Commons in order to suppress discussion of any alternative to its withdrawal agreement with the EU, the House changed the rules to deprive it of its exclusive control of the agenda. When the government of Mr Johnson tried to abuse its power to prorogue Parliament so as to suppress criticism of its own Brexit policy, Parliament responded by passing the so-called Benn Act, restricting its ability to go for a no-deal Brexit. These were remarkable demonstrations of the strength of our constitution's unwritten conventions. They also illustrated its ability to adapt to new challenges.

But what of the challenges of the next decade? Not all of them can be foreseen. But some can, and I propose to address three of those. The first is the twin problem of the electoral system and the narrow popular base of the major political parties. These two things are closely related, as I shall explain. The second is the constitutional role of the courts, and the future of judicial review. The third is the challenge of international lawmaking in a world where democracy is fundamentally national. These are not the only challenges that we will face over the next decade. In particular I omit the challenge of Scottish nationalism, which would require an essay in itself. But apart from that, the three that I have chosen seem likely to be the most important.

The government has committed itself to retaining the first-past-the-post system in general elections. Nonetheless, I address the electoral system and the role of political parties first, because these two things are fundamental to the government's professed objective of restoring trust between the electorate and professional politicians. Political parties have a critical function in a mass democracy. They mediate between the public and the state, in their search for a slate of policies that can attract the widest range of support and maximise their electoral prospects. They operate in what I have more than once called the political market. Their policies evolve in response to changing perceptions of what the electorate wants. For these reasons those policies are usually a compromise: not just a compromise between different groups within the same political party, but a compromise with the policy platforms of other parties. This is fundamental to the ability of a democracy to accommodate the broadest possible range of opinion and so enable us to live together in peace without the systematic application of force.

The political market can only work if the electorate has a real choice. If parties only occupy the extremes, as they have recently tended to do, the electorate's choices will be very limited. The current move to the extremes is mainly due to the small membership rolls of constituency associations, which can too easily be taken over by politically dedicated groups, as indeed they have been in both major national parties. The move to the extremes has been assisted by changes in the organisation of all parties, which have shifted power to constituency associations, notably in the choice of the leader. Constituency associations have immense power. They choose not just the party leader, but parliamentary candidates. Yet they are small and unrepresentative group-uscules. They are mainly made up of enthusiasts who feel strongly enough about their own political agenda to sacrifice much of their leisure in order to participate in them. This necessarily differentiates them from the rest of the electorate at large. There is no rational reason why the choices available to the electorate should be in the hands of these tiny groups. If the current disconnect between the public and the political class is to be addressed, this is where we have to start.

You might ask: what has this got to do with the electoral system? The answer is quite a lot. No party has achieved an absolute majority among the electorate for many years. Not

even Margaret Thatcher or Tony Blair in their heyday succeeded in doing that. The effect of the first-past-the-post
system is to exaggerate the effect of electoral swings, so that
a major national party that falls short of an absolute majority
in the electorate, may nevertheless enjoy an absolute majority in the House of Commons. This has great advantages.
It contributes to the power and stability of British governments and their capacity for decisive action. But it also makes
it exceptionally difficult for third parties to achieve a representation in the House of Commons that fairly reflects their
following in the electorate at large, unless, like the Scottish
National Party, they have a geographically concentrated
base. This did not matter so much when the two major
parties between them represented a broad cross-section of
the electorate. But it matters extremely if voters have to ask
themselves in the polling booths which party they hate least
because there are no other realistic choices. If parties are to
be representative of a broad range of opinion, policy compromises have to be made. If compromises are not made within
the political parties, then they must be made between them.
That will require more and smaller parties, in order to represent policy positions not covered by either the Conservative
or the Labour Party. Proportional representation has serious
drawbacks, but it would have the considerable advantage of
forcing both parties to broaden their appeal beyond their
ideological base or run the risk of losing support to smaller
parties. Unless political parties are reformed so as to diminish the power of their constituency associations, the case for
proportional representation may become overwhelming.

Let me now turn to the second constitutional hot potato,
namely the political role of the courts. The problem which
the government has identified is the use of judicial review as
'politics by other means'. This is apparently to be the main
item on the agenda of its proposed Constitution, Democracy

and Rights Commission. I discussed the political role of the courts in my Reith Lectures last year. The problem can be shortly stated. The courts no longer consistently distinguish between cases where a minister has no power to act, or to act for some particular purpose, and cases where the judge simply does not like the underlying policy. Most decisions of the courts on judicial review involve the uncontroversial application of long-standing legal principles. But there is a highly significant minority of cases that can fairly be described as 'politics by other means'. A statute may be judged insufficiently clear to bear a meaning to which the judges object. Or people may be judged to have a 'legitimate expectation' that prevails over government policy. The concept of irrationality, a well-established ground of objection to public authorities' decisions, may be stretched to encompass anything that the judge regards as unreasonable by his own lights. Policy decisions or public consultations may be found defective for not sufficiently addressing some objection entertained by the judge hearing the case. And so on. The problem is particularly acute in the highly sensitive areas of immigration control and social benefits.

These developments are relatively new. They began in the 1960s. They have given rise to concern for many years among politicians of both major political parties as well as among academics and quite a few judges. Those who would defend the current situation generally do so in one of two ways. Either they redefine democracy as a system of values of which they happen to approve; or else they criticise representative democracy itself on the grounds that it does not always achieve the results that they regard as desirable. But we all have to face one basic reality. We are only a democracy because ministers are answerable to Parliament for the formation and execution of policy. Parliament may not always be as effective as it should be. But the House of Commons is the only institutional means by which the electorate can influence policy. The appropriation by the courts of the right to decide where the public interest lies cuts across demarcation lines that are fundamental to the democratic state. Parliament is the proper forum for political opposition to the government. The courts are not. Their judges are not politically selected. Nor are they accountable to the electorate for what they do.

Dealing with the problem by legislation will not be straightforward. This is because the problem is not the legal principles themselves, most of which are perfectly sound, but the way in which judges have stretched them to cover cases in which they simply disagree with the ministerial decision in question. Legislation requires definition, and questions of degree commonly defy definition. The judiciary would be in a strong position to obstruct anything that seriously undermined the rule of law. But there is every prospect that judicial cooperation will be forthcoming if the measures proposed are reasonable and directed only to the more overtly political manifestations of judicial activism.

The third challenge that I can see coming is closely related. It is the growing impact on our lives of international treaties. Some treaties are dynamic sources of law. Examples are the treaties constituting the European Union and the European Convention on Human Rights. Other treaties create an international framework for political decision-making. Examples are the treaties constituting the World Trade Organization, North Atlantic Treaty Organization and various treaties on climate change. The effect of most such treaties is to transfer what were previously purely domestic functions and jurisdictions to supranational bodies standing outside the constitutional framework of the United Kingdom. As a middle-ranking political and economic power, the United Kingdom is not able to shape the world according to its own national priorities or to ignore trends that are gathering force in the rest of the world. But internationalism challenges long-established legal and constitutional structures. The reason is that states remain the basic political and constitutional unit for democratic decision-making, but on some major issues supranational bodies are the only effective agents for dealing with major challenges.

All this has important implications for traditional lines of accountability in a democracy. Democracy is fundamentally national. In a democracy, national institutions are accountable directly or indirectly to national electorates. Supranational institutions cannot be made accountable in the same way. If law is made or political issues decided at supranational level, there is a democratic deficit, which may be more or less serious depending on the issue. This was the main objection to the European Union by those who wished to leave it. It was to resolve this problem that the EU treaties created a supranational representative body, the European Parliament. But even former remainers (like me) must acknowledge that the experiment failed. The reasons for that exemplify the difficulty of creating a supranational democracy. Representative assemblies only work if people accept the legitimacy of their decisions even where they disagree. For that to happen, they must identify themselves with a political community that the assembly seeks to represent. In the case of the European Parliament they must regard themselves as having a European identity as powerful as, say, their British, French or German identity. All the evidence suggests that in ancient European nations, and certainly in Britain, only a small minority do, or ever did. National identities are powerful and becoming more so, while supranational ones are relatively weak. This is inherent in the whole culture of Europe, a region with some common values but characterised by distinctive linguistic, legal, social, religious and political traditions. There is, however, more to this than national differences. The whole tendency of public sentiment over the past few decades has been away from vast and remote units of government, and towards smaller and more local ones which may be less effective but with which people can more readily identify. This is the common background to the separatism of the Scots, the Catalans, the Flemings, the Ukrainians and many others. Brexit itself was essentially about identity. We should not write off this trend as mere nationalism or national aggression, as some people have done. It is really about people's sense of their own collective identity, which is among the most basic instincts of social beings. But however we decide to classify it, we might as well get used to it, because public hostility to remote units of government is not going to change in the foreseeable future.

This is not a plea for countries to make wholly autonomous decisions as if the rest of the world did not exist. In many areas of national policy, we have to make decisions at international level, because they are not going to work at any other. In others areas, the state is perfectly capable of making effective legislative or political decisions at national level. In that case, we need a very good reason for adopting a method of making decisions that circumvents democratic approval. Where proposals are made for the adoption of international norms, we need to look carefully at what these proposals add and what they take away. Let me illustrate my point with two contrasting examples.

The first is the European Human Rights Convention. Those of you who followed my Reith Lectures will be aware that I am not an admirer of international human rights law. The Human Rights Convention deals exclusively with matters that could equally well be resolved at national level with no loss of efficiency and with a great deal more sensitivity to our cultural and institutional traditions. Every right derived from the treaty or from the decisions of the European Court of Human Rights could just as effectively be conferred by domestic legislation without the need for a treaty, provided that there was sufficient democratic demand for it. As far as the United Kingdom is concerned, the Convention adds nothing except international uniformity. Constitutionally, its effect is to confer two significant powers on domestic and international courts. The first is the power to develop the rights laid down in the Convention by a process of extrapolation and analogy which has been devised and applied by the European Court of Human Rights in Strasbourg. The second is to confer on judges rather than elected politicians the power to decide difficult questions of public policy about when a Convention right must yield to some competing public interest, such as the prevention and detection of crime, national security and so on. It is obvious that this transfer of power has significant implications for the democratic character of our constitution.

The fact that Parliament has authorised it is not an answer. A democratic Parliament may authorise a new method of making legislative or political decisions, but it is still necessary to ask ourselves whether the new method is itself democratic. The proposed Constitution Commission will apparently consider (among other things) whether the Human Rights Act should be amended so as to reduce the impact of the Convention on national decisions about crime, security and what it calls 'effective government'. This has provoked much suspicion and criticism. I think that the suspicion and criticism are premature. A lot will depend on what they propose to replace it with. But in principle, it is difficult to see why MPs should not be the ultimate judges of where the public interest lies. That is what they are elected for.

At the other end of the spectrum, climate change is the paradigm case of an issue that is incapable of being dealt with at national level. National boundaries are meaningless in the face of a global problem of that order. In the long run, climate change is likely to become a growing source of international tension as countries club together to impose climate-change policies on others who object or would prefer to free ride on the efforts of their neighbours. There is, however, an inevitable tension between the international character of the problem and national lines of democratic accountability. We are going to have to develop international structures for making collective decisions in a way that national electorates will regard as legitimate. One must hope that national electorates will feel a stronger sense of common identity in relation to climate change than they do in relation to, say, the common agricultural policy. I think that there is a good chance that they will.

I want to end by making two points that apply to all proposals for constitutional reform. Both of them hark back to my opening observation about the weight of history. The first point is that we cannot afford to alter our constitution on a partisan basis. Constitutional change is not like other legislation. It determines the way in which we make collective decisions for our society. Over the years, those decisions will be made by governments of different political complexions. The essential cement of any society is a common loyalty to a way of making decisions, irrespective of whether we agree with the outcome. A partisan change that suited just one strand of opinion would not achieve this. Any constitutional process must accommodate dissent, debate and a diversity of values and opinions, including values and opinions that the government of the moment does not share. These things are not just rules of political decency. They are fundamental to the survival of the democratic state.

My second point is that in a society with established institutions, radical change cannot be achieved by a process of demolition and reconstruction. Overt hostility to other national institutions such as the judiciary, the civil service and the BBC, which are accused of obstruction but in fact merely stand for a diversity of opinion, is often presented as a way of getting things done. It is in reality a certain route to failure. It increases the resistance of powerful institutions which enjoy considerable public support. People tend to judge politicians by their tone at least as much as their substance. Abuse is not a useful tool of policy. Shouting and snarling provokes unnecessary hostility among the electorate, which will ultimately doom the whole project.

This essay carries forward the theme of the previous one. It was originally a lecture commissioned by the BBC as part of a series dealing with the future shape of British politics and society. It was delivered in March 2020 at King's College, London, and broadcast a few days afterwards. Unfortunately the rest of this imaginative project fell by the wayside as a result of the Covid-19 epidemic, which is the subject of the next essay.

GOVERNMENT BY DECREE: COVID-19
AND THE BRITISH CONSTITUTION

During the Covid-19 pandemic, the British state has exercised coercive powers over its citizens on a scale never previously attempted. It has taken effective legal control, enforced by the police, over the personal lives of the entire population: where they could go, whom they could meet, what they could do even within their own homes. For three months it placed everybody under a form of house arrest, qualified only by their right to do a limited number of things approved by ministers. All of this has been authorised by ministerial decree with minimal parliamentary involvement. It has been the most significant interference with personal freedom in the history of our country. We have never sought to do such a thing before, even in wartime and even when faced with health crises far more serious than this one.

It is customary for those who doubt the legality or constitutional propriety of the government's acts to start with a hand-wringing declaration that they do so with a heavy heart, not doubting for a moment the need for the measures taken. I shall not follow that tradition. I do not doubt the seriousness of the epidemic, but I believe that history will look back on the measures taken to contain it as a monument of collective hysteria and governmental folly. This evening, however, I am not concerned with the wisdom of this policy, but only with its implications for the government of our country. So remarkable a departure from our liberal traditions surely calls for some consideration of its legal and constitutional basis.

The present government came to office after the general election of December 2019 with a large majority and a good deal of constitutional baggage. It had not had an absolute majority in the previous Parliament, which had rejected its policy on the terms for leaving the European Union. It had responded to parliamentary opposition with indignation. The attorney-general told the House of Commons in September 2019 that they were unfit to sit, surely one of the more extraordinary statements ever made in public by a law officer of the Crown. The government had endeavoured to avoid parliamentary scrutiny of their negotiations with the EU by proroguing it, and had been prevented from doing so by the Supreme Court's decision in *Miller (No. 2)*. The ground for the court's intervention was that prorogation impeded the essential function of Parliament in holding the government to account. This decision was certainly controversial in expressing as a rule of law something that had traditionally been regarded as no more than a political convention, although I have no doubt for my part that the court was right. But whether it is properly classified as law or convention, the constitutional principle that the court stated was surely beyond question. Governments hold power in Britain on the sufferance of the elected chamber of the legislature. Without that, we are no democracy. As the court pointed out, the dependence of government on parliamentary support was the means by which 'the policies of the executive are subjected to consideration by the representatives of the electorate, the executive is required to report, explain and defend its actions, and citizens are protected from the arbitrary exercise of executive power'. The present government has a different approach. It seeks to derive its legitimacy directly from the people, bypassing their elected representatives. Since the people have no institutional mechanism for holding governments to account, other than Parliament, the effect is that ministers are accountable to no one, except once in five years at general elections.

Within four months of the election, the new government was faced with the coronavirus pandemic. The minutes of the meetings of SAGE, its panel of expert scientific advisers, record that shortly before the lockdown was announced the behavioural scientists advised against the use of coercive powers. 'Citizens should be treated as rational actors, capable of taking decisions for themselves and managing personal risk', they had said. The government did not act on this advice. Encouraged by the public panic and the general demand for action, it opted for a course which it believed would make it popular. It chose coercion. For this, it needed statutory powers.

There were three relevant statutes.

The Coronavirus Act was passed specifically to deal with Covid-19. This hefty document of 348 pages with 102 sections and 29 schedules was pushed through all its stages in a single day in each House as the lockdown was announced. In the time available, no serious scrutiny of its terms can have been possible. The Act was primarily concerned to enlarge the government's powers to marshal the medical resources of the country and to authorise additional public expenditure. But tucked away in Schedules 21 and 22 were additional powers to control the movement of people. Schedule 21 authorises public health officials to screen and test people for infectious diseases. They are given extensive powers to control the movement of anyone found to be infectious and to call on the police to enforce their directions. Schedule 22 confers on the secretary of state extensive powers to forbid 'events' or 'gatherings' and to close premises for the purpose of controlling the transmission of Covid-19. For present purposes, however, the important point to note is that apart from the power to prevent events or gatherings, the Act conferred no power to control the lives of healthy people. The measure stood in a long tradition dating back many centuries by which infectious diseases were controlled by the confinement of infectious people, not by the confinement of healthy ones.

A power to confine healthy people was, however, conferred by another Act, the Civil Contingencies Act 2004. The Civil Contingencies Act is the only statute specifically designed for emergencies serious enough to require the kind of measures that we have had. It authorises ministers to make regulations to deal with a wide variety of 'events or situations', including those that threaten 'serious damage to human welfare'. These are defined so as to include things which may cause loss of life or illness. The regulation-making power could not be wider. Ministers are authorised to do by regulation anything that Parliament could do by statute, i.e. anything at all. In other words, it authorises government by executive decree. Specific examples given in the Act include restricting the movement or assembly of people and controlling travel. In enacting these provisions, Parliament recognised that emergency legislation of this kind is constitutionally extremely dangerous. It therefore provided for the powers to be exercisable only under stringent parliamentary control. I shall return to that.

The government chose not to include a general lockdown power in the Coronavirus Act and not to use the power that it already had under the Civil Contingencies Act. Instead it resorted to the much more limited powers conferred by Part IIA of the Public Health (Control of Disease) Act 1984, as amended in 2008. Section 45C(1) authorises the secretary of state to make regulations 'for the purpose of preventing, protecting against, controlling or providing a public health response to the incidence or spread of infection or contamination in England and Wales'. That sounds very wide, but the problem about it is that the power is couched in wholly general terms. It is a basic constitutional principle that general words are not to be read as authorising the infringement of fundamental rights. The best-known formulation of what has been called the 'principle of legality' comes from the speech of Lord Hoffmann in *Ex parte Simms* [2000] 2 AC 115, 131. His words are well known, but they are so apposite as to be well worth repeating. Parliament, he said,

> must squarely confront what it is doing and accept the political cost. Fundamental rights cannot be overridden by general or ambiguous words. This is because there is too great a risk that the full implications of their unqualified meaning may have passed unnoticed in the democratic process. In the absence of express language or necessary implication to the contrary, the courts therefore presume that even the most general words were intended to be subject to the basic rights of the individual. In this way the courts of the United Kingdom, though acknowledging the sovereignty of Parliament, apply principles of constitutionality little different from those which exist in countries where the power of the legislature is expressly limited by a constitutional document.

There are few more fundamental rights than personal liberty. The effect of the principle of legality is that those proposing its curtailment must be specific about it and take the political heat.

So what *specific* powers to curtail personal liberty does the Public Health Act confer? The answer is that its main purpose is to confer extensive powers on magistrates to make orders in relation to particular people thought to be infectious or specific premises thought to be contaminated. Magistrates can make orders disinfecting infectious people, quarantining or isolating them or removing them to hospitals, among other things. They can order the closure or decontamination of contaminated premises. Ministers are given very limited powers in this area, only two of which were relevant to the lockdown or to current measures of social control. Under Section 45C they have a specific power to make regulations controlling 'events or gatherings'. A 'gathering' is not defined, but the context shows it to be concerned with more substantial assemblies than ordinary social interchange in people's homes. The object was to deal with threats to public order. Otherwise the only specific power conferred on ministers is a power to do some of the things that a magistrate could do. The result is that ministers can make regulations controlling people thought to be infectious. There is no specific power under the Act to confine or control the movements of healthy people. To interpret it as conferring such a power would not only be inconsistent with the principle of legality. It would also be contrary to the whole tenor of this part of the Act. It is axiomatic that if a statute deals in terms with the circumstances in which a power can be exercised so as to curtail the liberty of the subject, it is not open to a public authority to exercise the power in different or wider circumstances. The courts will, I suspect, be tempted to give the government more leeway than they are entitled to. But on well-established legal principles, the powers under the Public Health Act were not intended to authorise measures as drastic as those which have been imposed.

Why did the government not include a lockdown power in the Coronavirus Act, given that it was drafted at the inception of the crisis? The most plausible explanation is that it thought that there might be difficulty in getting such a thing through Parliament without further debate and possible amendment. Why did they not use the Civil Contingencies Act, which was already on the statute book? The most plausible answer is that the Civil Contingencies Act required a high degree of parliamentary scrutiny which ministers wished to avoid. Emergency regulations under the Civil Contingencies Act must be laid before Parliament in draft before they are made. If the case is too urgent for that, they must be laid before Parliament within seven days or they will lapse. If necessary, Parliament must be recalled. Even if the regulations are approved, they can remain in force for only thirty days unless they are renewed and reapproved. Unusually, Parliament is authorised to amend or revoke them at any time. By comparison, the degree of scrutiny provided for under the Public Health Act is limited. In urgent cases, regulations under the Public Health Act have provisional validity, pending parliamentary approval, for twenty-eight days, and that limit is extended for any period when Parliament is not sitting. Parliament cannot amend them, and once it has approved them it cannot revoke them. They remain in force for whatever period ministers may decide. These differences in the level of parliamentary scrutiny were remarked upon at the time when the powers in question were added to the Public Health Act in 2008. The government of the day told the Constitution Committee of the House of Lords that the lesser degree of parliamentary scrutiny was appropriate because the powers under the Public Health Act were not intended to authorise anything very radical. They were mainly directed at controlling the behaviour of infected people, and then only in cases where the proposed measure was urgent but 'minor in scope and effect'.

The problems begin with the very first days of the lockdown. In his televised press conference of 23 March, the prime minister described his announcement of the lockdown as an 'instruction' to the British people. He said that he was 'immediately' stopping gatherings of more than two people in public and all social events except funerals. A number of police forces announced within minutes of the broadcast that they would be enforcing this at once. The Health Secretary, Mr Hancock, made a statement in the House of Commons the next day in which he said: 'these measures are not advice; they are rules'. All of this was bluff. Even on the widest view of the legislation, the government had no power to give such orders without making statutory regulations. No such regulations existed until 1 p.m. on 26 March, three days after the announcement. The prime minister had no power to give an instruction to the British people, and certainly no power to do so by a mere oral announcement at a Downing Street press conference. The police had no power to enforce them. Mr Hancock's statement in the House of Commons was not correct. Until 26 March the government's statements were not rules, but advice, which every citizen was at liberty to ignore.

To complain about the gap of three days during which the government pretended that the rules were in effect when they were not may strike some people as pedantic. The regulations were eventually made, albeit late. But it revealed a cavalier disregard for the limits of their legal powers which has continued to characterise the government's behaviour. Over the following weeks the government made a succession of press statements containing what it called 'guidance', which went well beyond anything in the regulations. These statements had no legal status whatever, although this fact was never made clear. The two-metre distancing rule, for example, never had the force of law in England. Many police forces set about enforcing the guidance nonetheless, until the College of Policing issued firm advice to them that they had no business doing so.

Why did the government, once they had announced the lockdown on 23 March, wait for three days until the 26th before making their regulations, and then resort to the emergency procedure on the ground that it was so urgent that Parliament could not be consulted in advance? The obvious answer, I am afraid, is that Parliament adjourned for the Easter recess on the 25th. They deliberately delayed their urgent regulations so that there would be no opportunity to debate them before the recess. The period of twenty-eight days before any kind of parliamentary scrutiny was required was thus extended by the twenty-one days of the recess, i.e. to the middle of May.

This is not the only respect in which the level of parliamentary scrutiny of the executive has been curtailed. The Coronavirus Act authorises any payments connected with coronavirus without limit and without any form of advance parliamentary scrutiny. The Contingencies Fund Act, which passed through every stage in the House of Commons on the day after the Coronavirus Bill, authorised an increase in the statutory maximum in the Contingencies Fund, from 2 per cent of the previous year's authorised expenditure, to 50 per cent. The result was to make an additional £266 billion available to the government with no advance parliamentary scrutiny. These measures departed from a century and a half of constitutional principle by which Parliament controls exactly how public funds are spent.

There were a number of other steps radically affecting the rights of individuals which the government took without any parliamentary sanction. Most of these involved exploiting existing regulatory regimes. The two-metre distancing rule, for example, was uncritically adopted by the Health and Safety Executive. As a result, a number of building sites and factories, where it was impractical to observe it, were required to close although not included in the closure orders made under statutory powers. Perhaps the most remarkable example concerns the steps that the government took to deprive people of access to medical and dental services. The provision of medical and dental services was expressly excluded from the closure orders made under the Public Health Act. But a combination of government advice and government-inspired pressure from regulators was used to limit access to general practitioners. They were required to conduct video triages and refer serious cases to hospitals while telling other cases to wait. This has had a serious impact on the diagnosis and early treatment of far more mortal diseases than Covid-19, notably cancer. More drastic still were the steps taken to close down dental practices. On 25 March, the chief dental officer, a government official, published a statement referring to the prime minister's announcement of the lockdown and requiring dentists to stop all non-urgent activity. In reality, they were required to stop even urgent activity. Their role was limited to carrying out a video triage of patients. Urgent cases were to be referred to a small number of local urgent dental units which essentially performed extractions. Treatment was refused in other cases. This direction, which had no statutory basis, left many people in pain or discomfort and threatened a significant number of dental practices with insolvency. Even after it was lifted at the beginning of June, distancing rules were imposed which seriously reduced the number of patients that a dentist could see and made many dental practices financially unviable. This is a serious matter, because the government's use of non-statutory procedures like these escapes parliamentary scrutiny. Parliament may, for example, be taken to have approved, albeit seven weeks late, the exception in the Health Protection Regulations which allowed the provision of dental services to continue. Parliament has never had the opportunity to approve the instruction of the chief dental officer to the opposite effect.

These events give rise to concern on a number of counts. The most draconian of the government's interventions, with the most far-reaching economic and social effects, have been imposed under an Act that does not appear to authorise them. The sheer scale on which the government has sought to govern by decree, creating new criminal offences, sometimes several times a week on the mere say-so of ministers, is in constitutional terms truly breathtaking. The government has routinely made use of the exceptional procedure authorising it in urgent cases to dispense with advance parliamentary approval, even where the measure in question has been mooted for days or weeks. Thus the original lockdown was imposed without any kind of parliamentary scrutiny until the middle of May, seven weeks later. Thereafter, there was little scope for further scrutiny. Even the powers which the government purported to exercise were gratuitously expanded by tendentious and misleading 'guidance', generally announced at press conferences.

A special word needs to be said about the remarkable discretionary powers of enforcement conferred on the police. The police received power to enforce the lockdown regulations by giving directions to citizens which it was a criminal offence to disobey. Fixed penalty notices are normally authorised in modest amounts for minor regulatory infractions, parking and the lesser driving offences. The government's regulations, however, authorised them for a great variety of newly created offences and sometimes in very large amounts. On 26 August the government introduced by decree an offence of 'being involved' in a gathering exceeding thirty people, and empowered any policeman in the land to issue a fixed penalty notice of £10,000. This sum, enough to ruin most people, was far in excess of any fine that would be imposed by a court for such an offence. The power, which was originally advertised as being intended to deal with 'raves' has of course been widely exercised for other purposes. In particular, it has been used to suppress protests against the government's coronavirus policies. On 30 August, the police served a £10,000 fixed penalty notice on Mr Piers Corbyn for addressing a rally against masks in Trafalgar Square. The regulations contain an exception for political protest, provided that the organisers have agreed a risk assessment and have taken reasonable steps to ensure safety. On 26 September the police broke up a demonstration against the government's measures, the organisers of which had agreed a risk assessment and had taken reasonable steps. The police claim to have done this because some of the demonstrators had not acted in accordance with the arrangements made by the organisers. They cleared the square using batons with considerable violence, injuring some twenty people who were guilty of nothing other than attending an apparently lawful protest. There is a noticeable process of selection involved in these actions. No such fines, arrests or assaults have been seen in other demonstrations, such as those organised by Black Lives Matter, or Extinction Rebellion, which did not observe social distancing but were thought to have greater public support. The Mayor of London applauded the police action. The silence from civil rights organisations such as Liberty was deafening.

The police's powers of summary arrest are regulated by primary legislation, the Police and Criminal Evidence Act 1984. Under Regulation 9(7) of the original lockdown regulations, the government purported to amend that Act by enlarging their powers of arrest so that they extended to any case in which a policeman reasonably believed that it was necessary to arrest a citizen to maintain public health. I need hardly say that the Public Health Act confers no power on ministers to amend other primary legislation in this way.

In fact, the police substantially exceeded even the vast

powers that they received. In the period immediately after the announcement of the lockdown, a number of chief constables announced that they would stop people acting in a way that they regarded as inessential, although there was no warrant for this in the regulations. One of them threatened to go through the shopping baskets of those exercising their right to obtain supplies, so as to ensure that they were not buying anything that the constable might regard as inessential. Other forces set up road blocks to enforce powers that they did not have. Derbyshire police notoriously sent up surveillance drones and published on the internet a film clip denouncing people taking exercise in the Derbyshire fells, something which people were absolutely entitled to do. When I ventured to criticise them in a BBC interview for acting beyond their powers, I received a letter from the Derbyshire Police Commissioner objecting to my remarks on the ground that in a crisis such things were necessary. The implication was that in a crisis the police were entitled to do whatever they thought fit, without being unduly concerned about their legal powers. That is my definition of a police state.

Many people think that in an emergency public authorities should be free to behave in this way because the ordinary processes of lawmaking are too deliberate and slow. I do not share this view. I believe that in the long run the principles on which we are governed matter more than the way in which we deal with any particular crisis. They are particularly important in a country like ours in which many basic rights and liberties depend on convention. They depend on a recognition not just that the government must act within its powers, but that not everything that a government is legally entitled to do is legitimate. The Public Health Act requires any exercise of its regulation-making powers to be proportionate. The government has included in every regulation to date a formulaic statement that it is. But its actions speak differently. Its public position is explicable only on the basis that absolutely anything is justifiable in the interest of hindering the transmission of this disease. I reject that claim. Powers as wide and intrusive as those that this government has purported to exercise should not be available to a minister on his mere say-so. In a society with the liberal traditions of ours, the police ought not to have the kind of arbitrary enforcement powers that they have been given, let alone the wider powers that they have not been given but have exercised anyway. These things should not happen without specific parliamentary authority, in the course of which the government can be required to explain its reasons and the evidence behind them in detail, and its proposals can be properly debated, amended or rejected by a democratic legislature. Their imposition by decree, even if the decrees are lawful, is not consistent with the constitutional traditions of this country.

There are, I would suggest, at least three lessons to be learned from this dismal story.

The first lesson is one to which I drew attention in my BBC Reith lectures last year. Our society craves security. The public has unbounded confidence, which no amount of experience will dent, in the benign power of the state to protect them against an ever wider range of risks. In Britain, the lockdown was followed by a brief period in which the government's approval ratings were sky-high. This is how freedom dies. When societies lose their liberty, it is not usually because some despot has crushed it under his boot. It is because people voluntarily surrendered their liberty out of fear of some external threat. Historically, fear has always been the most potent instrument of the authoritarian state. This is what we are witnessing today. But the fault is not just in our government. It is in ourselves. Fear provokes strident calls for abrasive action, much of which is unhelpful or damaging. It promotes intolerant conformism. It encourages abuse directed against anyone who steps out of line, including many responsible opponents of this government's measures and some notable scientists who have questioned their empirical basis. These are the authentic ingredients of a totalitarian society.

The same is true, I regret to say, of another feature of the history, namely the propaganda by which the government has to some extent been able to create its own public opinion. Fear was deliberately stoked up by the government: the language of impending doom; the daily press conferences; the alarmist projections of the mathematical modellers; the manipulative use of selected statistics; the presentation of exceptional tragedies as if they were the normal effects of Covid-19; above all the attempt to suggest that Covid-19 was an indiscriminate killer, when the truth was that it killed identifiable groups, notably those with serious underlying conditions and the old, who could and arguably should have been sheltered without coercing the entire population. These exaggerations were not accidental; they followed naturally from the logic of the measures themselves. They were necessary in order to justify the extreme steps that the government had taken, and to promote compliance. As a strategy, this was completely successful. So successful was it that when the government eventually woke up to the damage it was doing, especially to the economy and the education of children, it found it difficult to reverse course. The public naturally asked themselves what had changed. The honest answer to that question would have been that nothing much had changed. The threat had not been fairly presented in the first place. Other governments, in Germany, in France, in Sweden and elsewhere, addressed their citizens in measured terms, treating them as adults, and the level of fear was lower. It is not fair to criticise the government for the mere fact that the death toll in Britain is the second highest in Europe. There are too many factors other than government action which determine the mortality of Covid-19. But it is fair to blame them for the fear which means that Britain seems likely to suffer greater economic damage than almost every other European country.

The ease with which people could be terrorised into surrendering basic freedoms which are fundamental to our existence as social beings came as a shock to me in March 2020. So has much of the subsequent debate. I certainly never expected to hear the word libertarian, which only means a believer in freedom, used as a term of abuse. Perhaps I should have done. For this is not a new problem. Four centuries ago the political theorist Thomas Hobbes formulated his notorious apology for absolute government. The basis of human society, he argued, is that people have no right to be free, for they completely and irrevocably surrender their liberty to an overpowering state in return for security. In an age obsessed with escaping from risk, this has become one of the major issues of our time.

I have criticised the way in which the government has invaded civil liberties with limited parliamentary scrutiny or none. But of course parliamentary scrutiny is not enough unless Parliament itself is willing to live up to its high constitutional calling. It has to be ready to demand rational explanations of ministerial actions and to vote down regulations if they are not forthcoming or not persuasive. There is unfortunately little evidence of this. The public's fear effectively silenced opposition in the House of Commons. The official opposition did not dare to challenge the government, except to suggest that they should have been even tougher even more quickly. Parliament allowed the Coronavirus Act to be steamrollered through with no real scrutiny. It agreed to go into recess at the critical point in March and April when the need for active scrutiny of government was at its highest. When it returned, it meekly accepted government guidance on social distancing, and submitted to a regime under which only fifty out of the 650 members could be in the Chamber at any one time with up to 120 more participating remotely on screens. This has meant that instead of answering to a raucous and often querulous and difficult assembly, whose packed ranks can test governments with the largest majorities, ministers had an easy ride. The exclusion of most of the House of Commons from participating in the core activities for which they had been elected by their constituents was a most remarkable abdication of the House's constitutional functions. It has reduced its scrutiny of the government to the status of a radio phone-in programme.

However, the basic problem is even more fundamental. Under its standing orders, the House of Commons has no control over its own agenda. Its business is determined by the Leader of the House, a government minister, and by the Speaker. Backbenchers, however numerous, have no say and the official opposition not much more. In this respect the Commons is unlike almost every other legislature in the world. Other legislatures determine their own agenda through bipartisan committees or rules which entitle members with a minimum level of support to move their own business. When, in September, MPs began to kick back against the government's dictatorial measures, the only way that they could do it was to tack a proviso on to a resolution authorising the continuance of the Coronavirus Act, requiring the government to obtain parliamentary approval of regulations made under the Public Health Act. The Speaker, probably rightly, ruled this out as an abuse. But it should not have been necessary to resort to devices like this. The standing orders date from another age when there was a shared political culture at Westminster which made space for dissenting views, and a shared respect for the institution of Parliament itself. The procedures of the House are not fit for a world in which the government seeks to shove MPs into the margins. Speaker Hoyle was surely right to accuse ministers of despising Parliament. But it will take more than schoolmasterly lectures to address the problem. Over the past few decades, the House of Commons has lost much of the prestige and public respect that it once enjoyed. Mr Cox's strictures against Parliament in September 2019 were outrageous. But Parliament will richly deserve them unless it can rise to the challenge of controlling the most determined attempt by any modern government to rule by decree.

So much for the first lesson of recent events. The second is a variant of Lord Acton's famous dictum that power corrupts and absolute power corrupts absolutely. Ministers do not readily surrender coercive powers when the need for them has passed. The Scott Inquiry into the Matrix Churchill scandal, which reported in 1996, drew attention to a broad class of emergency powers which had been conferred on the government at the outset of the Second World War until such time as His Majesty should declare by Order in Council that the war had ended. These had been kept in force by the simple device of ensuring that no such Order in Council was ever placed before His Majesty. They were still being used in the 1970s and 1980s on the footing that the Second World War was still in progress, for purposes quite different from those originally envisaged. Likewise, the powers conferred on ministers and the police by the Terrorism Acts of 2000 and 2006 have been employed not just to combat terrorism but for a variety of other purposes, including the control of peaceful demonstrations, the enlargement of police stop and search powers to deal with ordinary non-terrorist offences, and the freezing of the assets of an Icelandic bank for the protection of their UK depositors. It will therefore surprise no one that the present government, having announced on 23 March that the lockdown would last until the NHS was able to cope with peak hospitalisations, should have continued them in May and June after this objective had been achieved. Ministers did this notwithstanding the warning of their scientific advisers in reports submitted to SAGE in February and March that a lockdown could delay infections and deaths but not stop them. Once again, fear persuaded people to accept the surrender of their liberty, even when the lockdown was no longer capable of the objective originally claimed for it. If the government had made its regulations under the Civil Contingencies Act, as it should have done, they would have had to be reapproved by Parliament every thirty days. Even with a relatively supine House of Commons, it is permissible to hope that Parliament would at least have called for a coherent explanation of this pointless and profoundly damaging decision.

The third and last lesson which I want to draw from these events is that government by decree is not only constitutionally objectionable. It is usually bad government. There is a common delusion that authoritarian government is efficient. It does not waste time in argument or debate. Strong men get things done. Historical experience should warn us that this idea is almost always wrong. The concentration of power in a small number of hands and the absence of wider deliberation and scrutiny enables governments to make major decisions on the hoof, without proper forethought, planning or research. Within the government's own ranks, it promotes loyalty at the expense of wisdom, flattery at the expense of objective advice. The want of criticism encourages self-confidence, and self-confidence banishes moderation and restraint. Authoritarian rulers sustain themselves in power by appealing to the emotional and the irrational in collective opinion. The present government's mishandling of Covid-19 exemplifies all of these vices. Whatever one might think about the merits of its decisions, it is impossible to think well of the process that produced them, which can only be described as jerky, clumsy, inconsistent and poorly thought-out. There is not, and never has been, an exit plan or anything that can be described as a long-term strategy – only a series of expedients. The Public Accounts Committee of the House of Commons reported in July that the lockdown was announced without any kind of cost-benefit analysis or advance planning for its disruptive economic effects. The many relevant social and educational considerations were disregarded in favour of an exclusive concentration on public health issues and only some of those. These are all classic problems of authoritarian government. It is habitually ineffi-cient, destructive, blinkered and ultimately not even popular.

The British public has not even begun to understand the seriousness of what is happening to our country. Many of them, perhaps most, don't care, and won't care until it is too late. They instinctively feel that the end justifies the means, the motto of every totalitarian government which has ever been. Yet what holds us together as a society is precisely the means by which we do things. It is a common respect for a way of making collective decisions, even if we disagree with the decisions themselves. It is difficult to respect the way in which this government's decisions have been made. It marks a move to a more authoritarian model of politics which will outlast the present crisis. There is little doubt that for some ministers and their advisers this is a desirable outcome. The next few years are likely to see a radical and lasting trans-formation in the relationship between the state and the citizen. With it will come an equally fundamental change in our relations with each other, a change characterised by distrust, resentment and mutual hostility. In the nature of things, authoritarian governments fracture the societies they govern. The use of political power as an instrument of mass coercion is corrosive. It divides and it embitters. In this case, it is aggravated by the sustained assault on social interaction which will sooner or later loosen the glue that helped us to deal with earlier crises. The unequal impact of the government's measures is eroding any sense of national solidarity. The poor, the inadequately housed, the precariously employed and the socially isolated have suffered most from the government's measures. Above all, the young, who are little affected by the disease itself, have been made to bear almost all the burden, in the form of blighted educational opportunities and employment prospects, the effects of which will last for years. Their resentment of democratic forms, which was already noticeable before the epidemic, is mounting, as recent polls have confirmed.

The government has discovered the power of public fear to let it get its way. It will not forget. Aristotle argued in his *Politics* that democracy was an inherently defective and unstable form of government. It was, he thought, too easily subverted by demagogues seeking to obtain or keep power by appeals to public emotion and fear. What has saved us from this fate in the two centuries that democracy has subsisted in this country is a tradition of responsible government, based not just on law but on convention, deliberation and restraint, and on the effective exercise of parliamentary as opposed to executive sovereignty. But like all principles which depend on a shared political culture, this is a fragile tradition. It may now founder after two centuries in which it has served this country well. What will replace it is a nominal democracy, with a less deliberative and consensual style and an authoritarian reality which we will like a great deal less.

This piece was originally given as the annual Freshfields Law Lecture at Cambridge University in October 2020.

NOTES

1   *The Whig Interpretation of History* (1931).
2   *Prenn v Simmonds* [1971] 1 WLR 1381 and *Reardon Smith Line Ltd v Hansen-Tangen* [1976] 1 WLR 989.
3   *Antaios Compania Naviera v Salen Rederierna AB* [1985] AC 191.
4   *Sirius International Insurance Co v FAI General Insurance* [2004] 1 WLR 3251.
5   *Ford v Beech* (1848) 11 QB 852, 866.
6   [1997] AC 313.
7   [1998] 1 WLR 896.
8   [2009] 1 AC 1101.
9   [2011] 1 WLR 2100.
10 [2009] 1 WLR 1988.
11 [2016] AC 742.
12 [2015] AC 1619.
13 In the lecture, I deliberately avoided saying that *Rainy Sky* was wrongly decided. I felt inhibited because I was still a member of the Court, because some of my colleagues had been party to that decision, and because I might have to decide the question judicially in a future case. In the question and answer session which followed, I was put on the spot, and evaded the issue. Today, none of these considerations apply. In my view, *Rainy Sky* was wrong. The result contended for in *Rainy Sky* was not as odd as the result which we arrived at in *Arnold v Britton*.

I was party to *Arnold v Britton*, and I remain of the view that it set out the correct approach to a contract which was unfair but whose language clearly showed that it was what the parties intended.

14 [2017] UKSC 24.

15 *Nothman v London Borough of Barnet* [1979] I All ER 142.

16 *Council of Civil Service Unions and others v Minister for the Civil Service* [1985] AC 374.

17 Lord Hailsham, *Elective Dictatorship*, Dimbleby Lecture, BBC One, 14 October 1976.